D0072084

Beatniks

Guides to
Subcultures and
Countercultures

Beatniks

A Guide to an American Subculture

Alan Bisbort

GREENWOOD PRESS
An Imprint of ABC-CLIO, LLC

A B C 🔷 C L I O

Santa Barbara, California • Denver, Colorado • Oxford, England

Library of Congress Cataloging-in-Publication Data

Bisbort, Alan.
   Beatniks : a guide to an American subculture / Alan Bisbort.
       p. cm. — (Guides to subcultures and countercultures)
   Includes bibliographical references and index.
   ISBN 978-0-313-36574-4 (hard copy : alk. paper) — ISBN 978-0-313-36575-1 (ebook)
   1. Beat generation—History. 2. Subculture—United States. I. Title.
   PS228.B6B57   2010
   810.8′0054—dc22   2009031093

ISBN: 978-0-313-36574-4
EISBN: 978-0-313-36575-1

14 13 12 11 10   1 2 3 4 5

This book is also available on the World Wide Web as an eBook.
Visit www.abc-clio.com for details.

Greenwood Press
An Imprint of ABC-CLIO, LLC

ABC-CLIO, LLC
130 Cremona Drive, P.O. Box 1911
Santa Barbara, California 93116-1911

This book is printed on acid-free paper ∞

Manufactured in the United States of America

Copyright Acknowledgments

Quotations from *On the Road* in chapters 2 and 3 are reprinted by permission of SLL/Sterling Lord Literistic, Inc. Copyright by Jack Kerouac

The interview with Karl-Heinz Meschbach in chapter 4 was conducted by the author. Used with permission by Karl-Heinz Meschbach

The interview with Roy Harper in the conclusion was conducted by the author. It originally appeared as "Hats Off to Harper" in *Gadfly Online* magazine on October 1, 2001. Used with permission of Roy Harper.

The interview with Ann Charters in the biographical sketches section was conducted by the author. A portion of the interview originally appeared in the *Hartford Advocate* on April 27, 1995. Used with permission by the *Hartford Advocate*.

The interview with Allen Ginsberg (pp. 139–149) in the primary documents section was conducted by the author. A portion of the interview originally appeared in the *Hartford Advocate* on November 3, 1996. Used with permission by the *Hartford Advocate*.

The interviews with Allen Ginsberg (pp. 149–151) and Michael McClure in the primary documents section were conducted by Parke Puterbaugh. Used with permission by Parke Puterbaugh.

Contents

Series Foreword

From Beatniks to Flappers, Zoot Suiters to Punks, this series brings
to life some of the most compelling countercultures in American history. Designed to offer a quick, in-depth examination and current
perspective on each group, the series aims to stimulate the reader's
understanding of the richness of the American experience. Each book
explores a countercultural group critical to American life and introdu-
ces the reader to its historical setting and precedents, the ways in
which it was subversive or countercultural, and its significance and
legacy in American history. *Webster's Ninth New Collegiate Dictionary*
defines counterculture as "a culture with values and mores that run
counter to those of established society." Although some of the groups
covered can be described as primarily subcultural, they were targeted
for inclusion because they have not existed in a vacuum. They have
advocated for rules that methodically opposed mainstream culture, or
they have lived by their ideals to the degree that it became impossible
not to impact the society around them. They have left their marks,
both positive and negative, on the fabric of American culture.
Volumes cover such groups as Hippies and Beatniks, who impacted
popular culture, literature, and art; the Eco-Socialists and Radical

Feminists, who worked toward social and political change; and even groups such as the Ku Klux Klan, who left mostly scars.

A lively alternative to narrow historiography and scholarly monographs, each volume in the *Subcultures and Countercultures* series can be described as a "library in a book," containing both essays and browsable reference materials, including primary documents, to enhance the research process and bring the content alive in a variety of ways. Written for students and general readers, each volume includes engaging illustrations, a timeline of critical events in the subculture, topical essays that illuminate aspects of the subculture, a glossary of subculture terms and slang, biographical sketches of the key players involved, and primary source excerpts—including speeches, writings, articles, first-person accounts, memoirs, diaries, government reports, and court decisions—that offer contemporary perspectives on each group. In addition, each volume includes an extensive bibliography of current recommended print and nonprint sources appropriate for further research.

Preface

That's what the whole Beat Generation is, if it's anything—prophets
howling in the wilderness against a crazy civilization.

Allen Ginsberg, 1960 interview

In a way, it's a shame that such a vibrant and deeply influential
American counterculture as the one that was spawned by the Beat
Generation in the late 1940s would be boiled down in the minds of
millions to the stereotype of the "Beatnik." This easily recognizable
"type" is now as familiar to Americans of all ages as the "hippie,"
"punk" or "Goth": the men sporting goatees and/or Abe Lincoln
beards, striped sailor shirts or black turtlenecks, chinos, sandals,
berets, Ray-Ban sunglasses worn indoors and at night; the women
decked out in black, shape-enhancing sweaters, black tights, black
berets, black horn-rimed glasses, often barefoot, and given to spontaneous bursts of solo interpretive dancing. Bongo drums, Chianti bottles, and espresso cups can also be found scattered about the Beatnik
"pad" while improvised poetry and jazz flows freely.

Not that there's anything wrong with that, of course. . . .

This just was not what Jack Kerouac, Allen Ginsberg, William S.
Burroughs, Joan Adams (Burroughs), Gregory Corso, Herbert Huncke,

Lucien Carr, Neal Cassady, John Clellon Holmes, and all the others associated with the origin of the Beat Generation had in mind when they first ventured into the Manhattan night. Their goal was nothing less than a spiritual and cultural revolution—at a time when to be out of step in America was to be suspected of insufficient patriotism or even Communist tendencies. Indeed, by July 1960, the nation's most powerful political figure, FBI director J. Edgar Hoover, was fanning the final gusts of the Cold War by telling the Republican National Convention that the "three menaces" to America were "Communists, Beatniks and eggheads."

To those young people who read the novels and poems of Beat writers, viewed the paintings, sculptures, murals, and collages of Beat artists, gasped and gaped at Beat theater and dance troupes, and dug the Beat musical canon of Charlie Parker, Miles Davis, Dizzy Gillespie, and John Coltrane, these figures were the very opposite of "menaces." Indeed, for many they were saviors, providing a parallel and vastly more appealing culture and a way out of the Cold War conformity and consumerism.

All countercultural movements that have arisen since the Beats owe a debt to them, and some of the voices of those who were influenced by them are included in this book. Also included herein are some of the people, work, and happenings that have been neglected or given short shrift in other accounts of the Beat Generation. Among these are the women who shaped and were shaped by the Beat Generation, the scholars and facilitators, as well as the precursors by which the Beatnik counterculture was shaped.

Beatniks opens with a detailed timeline intended to convey the complexity, the myriad influences and events and places that belie the Beatnik stereotype. The narrative essay that follows ("Origins of the Beat Generation") offers historical context to the plethora of names and events in the timeline. Some further, more topical essays—"How the Beats Turned into Beatniks," "The Emergence of a Beatnik Voice," "Beatniks Take Manhattan, the Nation and the World"—focus on specific aspects of the counterculture. A series of biographical sketches charts the major and minor players, and a section of "primary documents" showcases their actual words, including exclusive interviews with Allen Ginsberg, Ann Charters, Roy Harper, and Michael McClure.

And what book called *Beatniks* would be complete without a glossary of the slang? Also included herein is an authoritative and detailed bibliography with recommended books, music, films, and Web sites for those who want to take their Beatnik fix to a multimedia level.

Acknowledgments

I thank Kristi Ward, popular culture acquisitions editor at Greenwood Press, who secured the contract for *Beatniks*, and George Butler, who took over the editing chores after the merger of Greenwood and ABC-CLIO. George offered invaluable suggestions and displayed commendable patience when the timeline proved to be ten pages longer than originally planned. I also once again thank Athena Angelos, picture researcher extraordinaire, for unearthing images from the collections of the Library of Congress; Tom Hearn, photographer extraordinaire, for lending me his talents to put together many of the images for this volume; and Sharon Hannon, author of the *Punks* volume in this series, for sharing strategies and good vibes. Finally, this book is dedicated to my own little homegrown Beatnik, Paul James Bisbort, the heir apparent to all of my archives.

Timeline

August 1940   18-year-old Jack Kerouac enrolls at Columbia University, where he has a football scholarship, breaking his leg in the second game of the season, which ends his football career.

Fall 1942   Kerouac accompanies Seymour Wyse to hear Charlie Parker and Dizzy Gillespie at Three Deuces on 52nd Street. Bebop jazz, which he called "a goofy new sound," would be the favored music of future Beats.

December 1942   Kerouac leaves Columbia University and joins the U.S. Navy.

May 1943   Kerouac receives an honorable discharge from the Navy for "indifferent character." While in the Navy he works on an unpublished novel, inspired by Herman Melville, called "The Sea Is My Brother."

Spring 1943   29-year-old William S. Burroughs moves from Chicago to New York City.

June–October 1943	Kerouac joins the Merchant Marines, surviving torpedo attacks by German U-boats and exploring England. The experience inspires him to dedicate his life to a literary project he dubs "the Duluoz Legend."
October–December 1943	Kerouac frequents New York's jazz clubs, where he regularly hears Billie Holiday, Art Tatum, Parker, Gillespie, and Slam Stewart.
December 1943	Kerouac and Columbia student Lucien Carr meet at the West End bar.
February 1944	William S. Burroughs and Kerouac meet.
March 1944	Allen Ginsberg, a 17-year-old Columbia freshman, seeks out Kerouac at Edie Parker's apartment, cementing a lifelong friendship.
August 13, 1944	Lucien Carr stabs David Kammerer to death, later claiming self-defense against a homosexual assault.
August 22, 1944	Kerouac marries Edie Parker at New York City Hall, partly to get out of the Bronx City Jail, where he is being held as a material witness to Kammerer's murder. The marriage was annulled less than two years later.
December 1944	Edie Parker and Joan Vollmer Adams get an apartment at 419 W. 115th Street.
March 16, 1945	Ginsberg is suspended for a year from Columbia for writing obscenities in the dust on his dorm window.
January 1946	Burroughs moves in with Joan Adams. The apartment now houses Edie Parker, Kerouac, Vicki Russell, and a Columbia student from Denver named Hal Chase.
December 1946	Neal Cassady and his wife, LuAnne Henderson, visit Hal Chase and Ed White, and meet Kerouac. The Beat Generation has its catalyst in Cassady.

January 1947	William and Joan Burroughs move to a farm in Texas, 50 miles north of Houston. Herbert Huncke joins them.
January 10, 1947	Kerouac introduces Cassady to Ginsberg and later describes the meeting in *On the Road*: "Two piercing eyes glanced into two piercing eyes. The holy con-man with the shining mind and the sorrowful poetic con-man with the dark mind."
March 4, 1947	Cassady leaves Manhattan, carrying a portable typewriter and vowing to take Kerouac's example to heart. The road now beckoned for the Beats.
July 17, 1947	Kerouac boards a bus to visit Cassady in Denver, and finds he and Ginsberg involved in an intense relationship. Cassady is also involved with Henderson and art student Carolyn Robinson. These confusing events would be included in Kerouac's novel *On the Road*.
August 30, 1947	Ginsberg and Cassady hitchhike from Denver to Burroughs's farm.
September 7, 1947	Ginsberg boards a coal-hauling ship in Houston bound for Africa before returning to New York and Columbia University.
Fall 1947	Ginsberg, inspired by artist Paul Cezanne's method of creating gaps in his images, begins creating "gaps" in his poems that "the mind would fill with the sensation of existence."
January 1, 1948	From Kerouac's journal: "Wrote 2500 words, until interrupted by a visit from Allen Ginsberg, who came at four o'clock in the morning to tell me he is going mad, but once and if cured he will communicate with other human beings as no one ever has—completely, sweetly, naturally."

June 1948	Ginsberg has a vision that William Blake read him his poem "Ah! Sunflower." Ginsberg says, "It was like God had a human voice, with all the infinite tenderness and mortal gravity of a living Creator speaking to his son." The vision makes Ginsberg believe "the spirit of the universe was what I was born to realize."
October 1948	Kerouac meets John Clellon Holmes; they spend hours at Holmes's apartment listening to Symphony Sid's radio show on WMCA ("six hours of nonstop bebop").
Thanksgiving 1948	Kerouac finishes a first draft of an early version of *On the Road*.
December 1948	Cassady returns to New York with ex-wife LuAnne Henderson and Al Hinkle to drive Kerouac to San Francisco. It was, wrote biographer Barry Miles, "the kind of pointless trip later celebrated by Kerouac in *On the Road*."
January 28, 1949	Kerouac, Cassady, Henderson, and Hinkle leave New York to begin the road trip that would shape later versions of *On the Road*. Their month-long "search for kicks" in New York was depicted in the novel *Go* by John Clellon Holmes.
February 1949	Kerouac takes a bus back to New York from San Francisco.
February 1949	Ginsberg allows the homeless Herbert Huncke to stay at his apartment. Huncke stays for two months; he and his criminal friends use Ginsberg's apartment to store stolen goods.
March 1949	Ginsberg shows Kerouac's manuscript for *The Town and the City* to his Columbia professor, Mark Van Doren, who recommends it to Robert Giroux at Harcourt Brace. The novel is accepted for publication.

March 30, 1949	On his 21st birthday, a suicidal Carl Solomon goes to the Columbia Presbyterian Psychiatric Institute and insists he wants a lobotomy.
April 22, 1949	Ginsberg is arrested for the stolen goods in his apartment.
June 29, 1949	Ginsberg voluntarily commits himself to the Columbia Presbyterian Psychiatric Institution, where he meets Carl Solomon, to whom he would dedicate "Howl."
August 28, 1949	Cassady returns to New York and gets a job parking cars.
September 1949	The Burroughs family moves to Mexico City.
January 13, 1950	Kerouac writes Ginsberg in the hospital to tell him, according to biographer Miles, "that he admired him, loved him, and considered him a great man. Such valuable friendship helped Allen to bolster his shattered ego and take charge of his life again."
February 27, 1950	Ginsberg is discharged from the hospital and moves in with his father and stepmother in Paterson, New Jersey, vowing to lead a "normal" life.
March 2, 1950	*The Town and the City*, Kerouac's first novel, is published.
March 4, 1950	Ginsberg writes William Carlos Williams a letter that says, in part, "I would like to make my presence in Paterson known to you, and hope you will welcome this from me, an unknown young poet, to you, an unknown old poet, who live in the same rusty county of the world." He also encloses nine poems. This initiates an important cross-generational friendship with two of America's most important poets.

March 1950	On a weekend trip to Manhattan, Ginsberg meets Gregory Corso, a 20-year-old self-taught poet, who has just left prison after serving a term for robbery.
October 17, 1950	Bill Cannastra, a mainstay of the Beat circle in New York, is killed when a prank on the subway backfires.
November 17, 1950	Kerouac marries dressmaker Joan Haverty, Cannastra's former girlfriend.
December 17, 1950	Kerouac receives the 13,000-word "Joan Anderson letter" from Cassady, which he would credit with helping to open up his own writing style. He writes Cassady, "I thought it ranked among the best things ever written in America."
April 2–22, 1951	Kerouac types the 125,000-word "scroll" of *On the Road*.
May 22, 1951	Kerouac writes Cassady about *On the Road*: "Plot, if any, is devoted to your development from young jailkid of early days to later (present) W. C. Fields saintliness. Book marks complete departure from Town & City and in fact from previous American literature."
August 1951	Ginsberg and Lucien Carr drive to Mexico City to visit the Burroughs.
September 6, 1951	Burroughs accidentally kills his wife, Joan, while trying to shoot a glass off her head.
October 25, 1951	Kerouac claims to have "discovered" spontaneous prose.
January 1952	Kerouac begins a five-month stay with the Cassadys in San Francisco.
January 1952	William Carlos Williams writes Ginsberg an encouraging letter.
February 16, 1952	Jack Kerouac's daughter, Jan, is born.

April 4, 1952	Ginsberg hand-delivers a copy of *Empty Mirror* to William Carlos Williams and the old poet tells him, "I guess this is an historical day."
May 18, 1952	Kerouac writes Ginsberg: "I know you will love *On the Road*—please read it all. . . . [It] is inspired in its entirety. . . . It is like *Ulysses* and should be treated with the same gravity."
July 1952	Ace Books pays Burroughs $1,000 advance for *Junkie* (later spelled "Junky").
Fall 1952	John Clellon Holmes's "Beat" novel *Go* is published.
November 13, 1952	Kenneth Patchen gives a reading at the San Francisco Museum of Art. "He stood very quietly, very ungiantlike, in the hush of concrete, with his cigarette, with his cane, like a blind man waiting for something. But he saw everything," writes Lawrence Ferlinghetti.
November 16, 1952	Holmes's article, "This is the Beat Generation," appeared in the *New York Times*, the first mention of "Beat" in any publication.
May 1953	*Junkie* (later *Junky*) is published as an "Ace Double" paperback, paired with *Narcotics Agent* by Maurice Helbrant. It would sell 113,170 copies by year's end.
August 1953	Burroughs returns to New York City to live with Ginsberg.
July 1953	Venerable literary critic Malcolm Cowley, an advisor to Viking Press, calls Kerouac "the most interesting writer who is not being published today."
October 1953	Kerouac writes *The Subterraneans* in 72 hours.
November 9, 1953	Dylan Thomas dies in New York's St. Vincent's Hospital. During the four days Thomas was in a coma, Corso snuck into the hospital to sit by his bedside.

December 30, 1953	*The Wild One* opens in New York. Marlon Brando portrays Johnny Strabler, a black leather-jacketed biker gang leader, the first cinematic treatment of the 1950s "antihero."
January 1954	Kerouac begins studying Buddhism, inspiring Ginsberg to do so, too.
February 8, 1954	Kerouac visits Neal and Carolyn Cassady in San Jose.
March 1954	Robert Creeley moves to Black Mountain, North Carolina, to teach and to edit an influential, if short-lived, Beat literary journal, the *Black Mountain Review.*
December 1954	Ginsberg meets Peter Orlovsky.
January 1955	Lawrence Ferlinghetti becomes sole proprietor of City Lights Pocket Book Shop in San Francisco, the center of the city's hip community.
January 22, 1955	The first "Poets' Follies" is held in San Francisco, organized by Weldon Kees, who hires a stripper to read T. S. Eliot while disrobing.
February 3, 1955	Ginsberg and Orlovsky get an apartment at 1010 Montgomery Street; Ginsberg would write his most famous poem, "Howl," there.
April 1955	*New World Writing* (Vol. 7) publishes Kerouac's "Jazz of the Beat Generation."
August 1955	Ginsberg writes "Howl."
August 10, 1955	City Lights Pocket Poet series releases the first of its important titles of Beat literature, *Pictures of a Gone World* by Lawrence Ferlinghetti.
September 8, 1955	At Kenneth Rexroth's suggestion, Ginsberg meets poet Gary Snyder in Berkeley. Snyder, a Zen Buddhist, would become the model for "Japhy Ryder" in Kerouac's novel *The Dharma Bums.*

September 9, 1955   Kerouac meets Snyder and Philip Whalen, who would remain among his closest friends and confidants until his death in 1969.

October 13, 1955   Six Beat poets (Michael McClure, Gary Snyder, Philip Lamantia, Philip Whalen, Lew Welch, and Allen Ginsberg) read at San Francisco's Six Gallery—an event Ginsberg called a "remarkable collection of angels all gathered at once in the same spot." Kerouac hails it as "the birth of the San Francisco Poetry Renaissance."

October 27, 1955   *Rebel Without a Cause* is released and America's youth find a cinematic hero in James Dean.

January 15, 1956   Kerouac finishes writing *Visions of Gerard* after 12 days, calling the "novel" about his dead brother "a full-length book of sorrows" and "my best book."

March 1956   Burroughs kicks heroin with help from doctors in England.

Spring 1956   The legendary Six Gallery reading of the previous October is reprised at a gallery in Berkeley. Ginsberg reads the entirety of "Howl."

May 5, 1956   Gary Snyder leaves for Japan to study Zen Buddhism.

June 1956   Kerouac hitchhikes to Desolation Peak to begin a 63-day stint as a fire watcher. The experiences shape his *Desolation Angels* (1965).

September 2, 1956   *The New York Times* runs Richard Eberhart's article "West Coast Rhythms," which brings national attention to the thriving poetry scene in San Francisco.

October 30, 1956   During a reading of "Howl," Ginsberg and Corso (also reading) are provoked by a heckler. Corso tells the heckler "Let's fight with words . . . images, metaphors, magic." Ginsberg disrobes, telling the startled gathering, "The poet always stands naked before the world."

December 21, 1956   Kerouac is invited to stay overnight in Washington, D.C., with U.S. poet laureate Randall Jarrell, who was hosting Corso. Kerouac paints a "surrealistic cat" for Jarrell and in exchange, Jarrell gives Kerouac a coat, sweater, and cap for his planned trip overseas. Jarrell tells Kerouac that *The Subterraneans* novel will be popular, giving Kerouac an important morale boost.

January 8, 1957   Kerouac delivers the manuscript of *On the Road* to Malcolm Cowley at Viking.

February 1957   *Mademoiselle* publishes an article on the San Francisco scene, "Flaming Cool Youth of San Francisco Poetry," bringing the Beats more national attention.

February 15, 1957   Kerouac leaves for Morocco, borrowing passage money from Ginsberg. While in Tangier, he types Burroughs's novel, *Naked Lunch*, also providing the title.

March 1957   Ginsberg and Orlovsky visit Burroughs and Kerouac in Tangier.

Spring 1957   The first issue of the *Evergreen Review* is published. The second issue, published in the summer of 1957 and called "The San Francisco Scene," would be one of the most important in Beat Generation literature, containing Kerouac's "October in the Railroad Earth," Ginsberg's "Howl," Henry Miller's "Big Sur and the Good Life," and poems by Ferlinghetti, Robert Duncan, Michael McClure, Josephine Miles, Jack Spicer, Gary Snyder, and Philip Whalen.

March 25, 1957	Chester MacPhee, collector of customs in San Francisco, seizes 520 copies of Allen Ginsberg's *Howl and Other Poems*, calling it "obscene."
April 16, 1957	The landmark recording *Thelonious Monk with John Coltrane* is released, soon becoming a staple of Beatnik album collections.
May 21, 1957	City Lights store manager Shigeyoshi Murao is arrested for selling a copy of *Howl and Other Poems* to an undercover police detective. As word of this ban spreads, the demand for the book of verse increases exponentially.
June 1957	Thelonious Monk begins a seven-month residency at the Five Spot, an East Village jazz club. His band includes John Coltrane. Their extended gig would be the musical event of the year for jazz aficionados.
Summer 1957	Norman Mailer's "The White Negro" essay is published in *Dissent*.
August 1957	The final issue of the *Black Mountain Review* is published, containing work by many Beat writers, including Kerouac, Ginsberg, Corso, Burroughs, Snyder, Philip Whalen, Robert Duncan, Philip Lamantia, Denise Levertov, and Hubert Selby Jr.
September 5, 1957	*On the Road* gets a lavish review in the *New York Times*.
September 25, 1957	Jack Kerouac appears on John Wingate's TV show *Nightbeat*, where 40 million viewers hear him respond to "What exactly are you looking for?" with "I'm waiting for God to show me His face." He called the Beats "a religious generation."
October 1957	Ginsberg and Orlovsky move to the Beat Hotel in Paris.

October 3, 1957	Judge Clayton Horn rules that the ban on "Howl" violates Ginsberg's First and Fourteenth Amendment rights.
November 13, 1957	Ginsberg begins writing "Kaddish," a long poem for his mother. Though "Howl" would remain his best-known poem, "Kaddish" was considered by many his greatest.
December 9, 1957	Kerouac finishes writing *The Dharma Bums*.
December 15, 1957	Kerouac emcees the first jazz poetry reading in New York, with David Amram, Howard Hunt, and Philip Lamantia participating, at the Brata Art Gallery on East 10th Street on a rainy night with no advance notice. It is packed.
December 19, 1957	Kerouac begins a weeklong gig at the Village Vanguard. Though his performances are criticized, TV personality and musician Steve Allen is impressed and suggests that he and Kerouac collaborate on recordings. Kerouac writes Ginsberg, "Read like a Zen lunatic saint, like you said to do."
January 1958	Burroughs moves to the Beat Hotel in Paris and begins "cut up" experiments with Brion Gysin.
January 20, 1958	Kerouac tells Mike Wallace on ABC-TV's *Night Beat* that the Beat philosophy was "a revival prophesied by [Oswald] Spengler. He said that in the late moments of Western civilization, there would be a great revival of religious mysticism. . . . We're all in Heaven now, really."
February 1958	John Clellon Holmes's "The Philosophy of the Beat Generation" is published in *Esquire*.
February 1958	Grove Press publishes Kerouac's *The Subterraneans*. In his preface to the novel, Henry Miller writes, "He's hot, red hot. And if he's

far out, he's also near and dear, a blood brother, an alter ego. He's there, everywhere, in the guise of Everyman."

March 1958   LeRoi and Hettie Jones begin publishing *Yugen*, an influential journal.

March 1958   Kerouac responds in *Esquire* to Holmes's "The Philosophy of the Beat Generation." "The sad thing is," writes Kerouac, "that while I am asked to explain the Beat Generation, there is no actual original Beat Generation left."

March 1958   Kerouac records his reading of "October in the Railroad Earth," "Wheel of the Quivering Meat Conception" and *Mexico City Blues*, with Steve Allen accompanying him on piano. *Poetry for the Beat Generation* (Hanover LP) is released in 1959.

April 2, 1958   Herb Caen coins "Beatnik" in his *San Francisco Chronicle* column.

April 8, 1958   Neal Cassady is arrested with three joints and for using his job as a railroad brakeman to smuggle pot.

May 11, 1958   The last "Poets' Follies" is held at Fugazi Hall in San Francisco. Billed as a "Bohemian Revel" and "session of S.F.'s unique Institution of Lower Learning," the event features "Beat Music."

July 4, 1958   Cassady begins his five-year sentence at San Quentin State Prison. He will be released early, on June 3, 1960.

October 15, 1958   Kerouac's novel *The Dharma Bums* is published.

November 6, 1958   Brandeis sponsors a "debate" on "Is There a Beat Generation?" with Kerouac and Ginsberg on the panel. Kerouac tells the crowd, "Live your lives out, they say; nah, love your lives out, so when they come around to stone you, you won't be living in any glass houses— only glassy flesh."

1959
The profile of the Beatnik reaches its peak, thanks largely to Maynard G. Krebs, the resident Beatnik on the television series *The Many Loves of Dobie Gillis*.

January 2, 1959
Alfred Leslie begins filming *Pull My Daisy* in his Bowery loft, with Robert Frank handling cinematography, David Amram composing the music, and Kerouac and Ginsberg cowriting the lyrics to the theme song.

February 2, 1959
Time runs a feature on the Beats in which Ginsberg is called "author of a celebrated chock-full catalogue called "Howl" . . . recognized leader of the pack of oddballs who celebrate booze, dope, sex and despair and go by the name of Beatniks."

February 5, 1959
Ginsberg gives a reading at Columbia, joined by Corso and Orlovsky. Kerouac is scheduled but does not show up. Ginsberg impresses a skeptical Diana Trilling, whose essay about the occasion, "The Other Night at Columbia," begins the process of gaining academic respect for selected Beat writers.

March 1959
The first issue of *Big Table* is published in Chicago, containing excerpts from the controversial *Naked Lunch*.

March 2, 1959
Miles Davis's sextet (John Coltrane, Cannonball Adderly, Paul Chambers, Jimmy Cobb, Bill Evans, Wynton Kelly) enters Columbia Records' 30th Street Studio to record one of the great works of the Beatnik canon, *Kind of Blue*.

April 1959
Kerouac's first column for *Escapade* appears, devoted to "The Beginning of Bop." Future

columns would be about Beat writers, baseball, and "the future of jazz," in which he called Thelonious Monk "the greatest composer who ever lived."

June 25, 1959   The Dave Brubeck Quintet releases their best-known album, *Time Out*, which features one of the few jazz compositions to ever be a hit single. "Take Five," written by saxophonist Paul Desmond, became a Beatnik signature song.

July 1959   *Naked Lunch* is published by Olympia Press.

July 3, 1959   A "Beatnik" exploitation film, *The Beat Generation*, was released.

August 3, 1959   CBS-TV airs *Raid in Beatnik Village*, a docudrama about police going undercover as Beatniks to "snare addicts and drug pushers of Greenwich Village."

September 29, 1959   The first episode of *The Many Loves of Dobie Gillis* airs on CBS. The situation comedy chronicles the high school hijinks and fantasies of the title character, whose best friend is the memorable Maynard G. Krebs, the first "Beatnik" character on network TV. The show will run until September 18, 1963.

November 11, 1959   The Beat film *Pull My Daisy* premieres in New York.

November 13, 1959   Ginsberg reads "Howl" at the Living Theatre in New York.

November 16, 1959   Jack Kerouac appears on *The Steve Allen Plymouth Show*, reading to millions from *Visions of Cody*, a book that would not be published in its entirety until after his death. The same night, *The Danny Thomas Show* on CBS-TV features a Beatnik character in an episode called "Terry Goes Bohemian."

November 30, 1959	*Life* runs an "exposé," "Beats: Sad but Noisy Rebels," that ends, "A hundred million squares must ask themselves: 'What have we done to deserve this?'" Reprinted in *Reader's Digest*, the piece spawned the image of Beats as "talkers, loafers, passive little con men, lonely eccentrics, mom-haters, cop haters, exhibitionists."
December 3, 1959	*The Betty Hutton Show* on CBS-TV airs an episode called "Art for Goldie's Sake," where Hutton crashes a party in a Beatnik disguise.
December 10, 1959	After a cross-country drive from San Francisco to New York, Lew Welch, Albert Saijo, and Jack Kerouac relax at photographer Fred McDarrah's pad.
December 22, 1959	A Los Angeles vice squad officer posing as a Beatnik investigates a mural at a Venice Beach coffeehouse after an obscenity complaint is filed.
February 6, 1960	*Saturday Review* carries a vicious attack in which John Ciardi claims, "The Beats are sprung out of a generation that had it easy."
April 15, 1960	The Living Theatre hosts a party in New York for Seymour Krim's acclaimed anthology, *The Beats*. At the event are Norman Mailer, Jack Micheline, Allen Ginsberg, Lawrence Ferlinghetti, Hubert Selby Jr., and LeRoi Jones.
April 20, 1960	Bob Hope and James Garner do a "comedy sketch" about Beatnik musicians on NBC-TV's *Bob Hope Buick Show*. The pair sings "The Will to Fail."
June 3, 1960	Neal Cassady is released from San Quentin State Prison after serving 787 days for a marijuana possession charge. By late 1962, Cassady would meet Ken Kesey and become one of the Merry Pranksters, forerunners of the hippies.

June 23, 1960	The movie version of Kerouac's *Subterraneans* is released.
July 20, 1960	A Beatnik Party announced its candidates and platform for the 1960 national elections. One of the candidates is Gnomi Gross, "Miss Beatnik of Chicago."
July 25, 1960	FBI Director J. Edgar Hoover tells the Republican National Convention that the "three menaces" to America are "Communists, Beatniks and eggheads."
September 1960	*Mad* magazine runs a six-page spoof of the "Beat Generation" that includes such features as "The Most Unforgettable Weirdo I've Met."
July 1962	Neal Cassady appears at Ken Kesey's house in Palo Alto, California, hoping to meet the author of the recently published *One Flew Over the Cuckoo's Nest*.
June 14, 1964	Ken Kesey's Merry Pranksters embark on a cross-country bus trip, from La Honda, California (near San Francisco) to New York, to launch the publication of Kesey's new novel, *Sometimes A Great Notion*. Neal Cassady—now nicknamed "Speed Limit"—is behind the wheel for a new generation of bohemians.
February 1965	The Fugs (Tuli Kupferberg, Ed Sanders, Ken Weaver) perform at the grand opening of the Peace Eye Bookstore, decorated by Andy Warhol, in New York's East Village. William Burroughs attends the opening. Steve Weber and Peter Stampfel of the Holy Modal Rounders are backup musicians at the event, which also draws guests as unlikely as George Plimpton and James Michener.
June 11, 1965	An important "International Poetry Reading" is held, filmed, and recorded at the Royal Albert Hall in London featuring Beat poets

	Allen Ginsberg, Gregory Corso, and Lawrence Ferlinghetti, along with poets from Russia and Europe.
January 14, 1967	The Human Be-In takes place in Golden Gate Park near Haight-Ashbury in San Francisco. Ferlinghetti and Ginsberg, passing the Beat Generation baton along to the burgeoning hippie generation, attend.
January 8, 1968	*Sports Illustrated* publishes an excerpt from Kerouac's *Vanity of Duluoz*. The introduction to the piece begins, "Years before he became a spokesman for the Beat Generation of the mid-1950s, the author was a promising football player."
February 4, 1968	Neal Cassady is found dead beside railroad tracks in Mexico.
February 5, 1968	*Vanity of Duluoz* is published, Kerouac's last book before his death.
September 1968	Kerouac appears on conservative William F. Buckley Jr.'s TV show, *Firing Line*, along with Ed Sanders and sociologist Lewis Yablansky. Kerouac agrees with Buckley that the hippies are part of the same "Dionysian movement" that infused the Beats, saying, "The hippies are good kids, they're better than the Beats."
October 21, 1969	Jack Kerouac dies in St. Petersburg, Florida, the birthday of Dizzy Gillespie, one of his favorite bebop musicians.

CHAPTER ONE

Narrative History: Origins of the Beat Generation

When the editors of the *Random House Dictionary* needed a definition of "Beat Generation" in 1960, they sought out novelist Jack Kerouac. And why not? After his 1957 novel *On the Road* became a cultural phenomenon—soon followed by the bestselling *The Dharma Bums* and *The Subterraneans*—Kerouac had been crowned "King of the Beats" by the media, which now deferred to him, or to poet Allen Ginsberg, on all matters pertaining to the Beat Generation or "Beatniks." Kerouac's response to Random House was this definition: "Members of the generation that came of age after World War II, who, supposedly as a result of disillusionment stemming from the Cold War, espouse mystical detachment and relaxation of social and sexual tensions."[1]

As authoritative as this definition may sound to the unenlightened, Kerouac cut some corners arriving at it. Indeed, before such a movement could embrace an entire "generation"—and then be elevated to a cultural "type" such as the "Beatnik"—it had to begin on a personal level. In this case, it began in New York City in the mid- to late 1940s, and grew out of a close friendship between three main players: Kerouac, a French Canadian football player, Merchant Marine, and aspiring novelist from working-class Lowell, Massachusetts; Allen

Ginsberg, a precocious Jewish poet from Paterson, New Jersey, attending Columbia University on a scholarship; and William S. Burroughs, an aristocratic Harvard graduate from St. Louis living off a family trust fund. Later, the circle widened to include poet Gregory Corso, who was born in Greenwich Village and grew up on the streets of New York; human dynamo Neal Cassady from Denver; Zen-practicing poet and naturalist Gary Snyder; novelist John Clellon Holmes; publisher-poet Lawrence Ferlinghetti; and many others within the circles of these figures—poets, playwrights, novelists, critics, painters, sculptors, dancers, actors, musicians, photographers, and filmmakers.

Kerouac first broached the idea of a separate "generation" with John Clellon Holmes in November 1948 during one of their late-night rap sessions. Kerouac and his friends Holmes, Ginsberg, Burroughs, Bill Cannastra, Lucien Carr, Hal Chase, Henry Cru, and many others haunted Manhattan's seedier areas, including Times Square and 42nd Street (then a string of erotic cinemas, strip clubs, and peep shows), where they rubbed shoulders with addicts, crooks, prostitutes, and other creatures of the night. The group first heard the then-slang term "beat" from Herbert Huncke, a junkie and petty thief who held court at a 24-hour automat where the city's marginal populations nursed cups of coffee to get out of the cold. Huncke's favorite expression was "Man, I'm beat." Though he later explained, "I meant beaten . . . the world against me," Kerouac found a deeper, more religious meaning in Huncke's weary plaint.[2]

Holmes later recalled that Kerouac tried to explain to him how the new generation had absorbed this "beat" feeling of Huncke's. "It's a kind of furtiveness," Holmes reported Kerouac (under the alias Gene Pasternak) saying in his 1952 novel *Go.* "Like we were a generation of furtives. You know, with an inner knowledge there's no use flaunting on that level, the level of the 'public,' a kind of beatness—I mean, being right down to it, to ourselves, because we all really know where we are—and a weariness with all the forms, all the conventions of the world. . . . So I guess you might say we're a 'beat generation.'"[3]

Kerouac and his kindred spirits were fascinated with more than Huncke's hip lingo. Kerouac particularly liked the "melancholy sneer" in his voice, as it inspired him to create "characters of a special spirituality who didn't gang up but were solitary Bartlebies staring out the dead wall window of our civilization."[4] Bartleby, the title character from Herman Melville's "Bartleby, the Scrivener," set in the Manhattan of a century earlier, was an iconic figure for the Beats. When asked to do something by his boss, Bartleby would reply, in a world-weary voice, "I would prefer not to." Kerouac combined Melville's evocative story with Huncke's ghostly appeal. And he and his friends shared with Huncke this sense of being "beat" or "beaten down," a state of psychological rawness and exhaustion that forced them to be completely open with one another. Kerouac, a devout Roman Catholic, soon expanded this initial sense of "Beat" to include his own spiritual and confessional yearnings. "Beat" to him meant beatitude, a state of transcendent spiritual bliss. He suggested that this could be attained not just in traditional places of worship but also by losing oneself in jazz, meditation, nature, art, and language, as well as through the sensory experiences of sex, alcohol, and/or drugs.

In 1992 Huncke told a *New York Times* reporter,

> I was a catalyst. I was more of a hipster than they [Kerouac and his friends] were. They were college kids holding collegiate discussions. To say that I was as hip as someone like Charlie Parker would be really stupid but I was pretty hip for a white guy. They were going around saying "hep" until I came along. I brought a whole new lexicon and they were interested in language. Take the word "beat." I would use it a lot. Eventually, it got to be used to describe the group as beatific. But when I used it, I meant tired, exhausted, beat down to your socks. It caught on.[5]

Another trait the three original Beats shared, which also came to be associated with the "Beatniks," was their lack of firm roots,

---

While living in New York, Allen Ginsberg, Jack Kerouac, and William S. Burroughs were all interviewed by Dr. Alfred Kinsey and their perspectives were incorporated in *Sexual Behavior of the Human Male* (1948). Kinsey's 15-year survey of attitudes and statistics changed the way Americans viewed sexuality.

restlessness, and inability to commit to anything or anyone. The trio met through mutual friend Lucien Carr in 1945–1946. Kerouac had been discharged from the Navy and was drifting aimlessly in search of inspiration for his unpublished novels. Ginsberg, a poet given to mystical visions and manic bursts of inspiration, was still enrolled at Columbia University but would soon be expelled, found guilty by association with a group of thieves (including Huncke) and sent to a mental hospital. Burroughs, eight years older than Kerouac and twelve years older than Ginsberg, had drifted to New York after unsuccessful graduate studies in Europe and Chicago, where he had also been a private detective and insect exterminator. His forays into the drug and criminal milieu on the fringes of Manhattan's nightlife led to his own addiction to heroin.

By the spring of 1946, the three men were sharing a four-bedroom apartment near Columbia University's campus in upper Manhattan. Burroughs lived in one room with his future wife, Joan Adams, and Kerouac lived with his future wife, Edie Parker, while Hal Chase and Allen Ginsberg were frequent overnight guests in the spare rooms. The group would have marathon discussions led by Burroughs, whose wide reading in psychology, anthropology, and European literature introduced the others to Oswald Spengler's *The Decline of the West*, Wilhelm Reich's theories of sex repression, Louis-Ferdinand Celine's free-form novels, and Jean Genet's outlaw writings.

The catalyst for this small circle to "hit the road" was Neal Cassady. A high school dropout and car thief from Denver, Cassady came to New York with his young wife, LuAnne Henderson, in December 1946. During that month-long visit, Cassady crossed paths with Kerouac, Ginsberg, and Burroughs; none were left unaffected by the meetings. The autodidactic Cassady possessed boundless energy and charisma and, despite his lack of schooling, a prodigiously active intellect. His frenetic restlessness infused them all. He was like a raw physical force that inspired action in these more bookish big-city bohemians. Indeed, after Cassady returned to Denver in January 1947, the rest of the Beat circle was infected by his wanderlust. Soon Burroughs moved with wife Joan to a farm in Texas, while Kerouac and Ginsberg visited Cassady in Denver. The events that would comprise the narrative of Kerouac's novel *On the Road*, the best-known work of Beat literature (though it would not be published until 1957), were set in motion.

Pre-Beatnik Bohemians

Making blanket statements about the Beat "movement" while it was unfolding in "real" time was nearly impossible, mainly because the whole thing began among a tight-knit group of friends who shared some of the same interests (Melville, Dostoevsky, Thomas Wolfe, Walt Whitman, surrealism, bebop jazz, Charles Baudelaire, Arthur Rimbaud). The Beats did not appear out of nowhere or exist in a vacuum. In the 1940s New York City possessed a storied history of bohemianism and unconventionality. Although the Left Bank of Paris is most often associated with bohemians—due in part to Henri Murger's book *Scenes de la vie de Boheme* (1848) and Puccini's opera *La Boheme* (1898), as well as to the city's long-lived and Siren-like appeal to artists—America played host to some thriving bohemian scenes. The best known were in New York (Greenwich Village and Harlem), Chicago, and the San Francisco Bay Area.

America's "Bohemia" began in earnest in New York in the 1920s, led by the likes of John Reed, Louise Brooks, Edna St. Vincent Millay, Eugene O'Neill, and Maxwell Bodenheim. Before he became the playboy-revolutionary depicted by Warren Beatty in the film *Reds*, John Reed (1887–1920) was the bohemian poet of Greenwich Village. While the Village emerged as America's Left Bank, Harvard graduate Reed chose the carefree life of the artist and applied his writing talents to documenting it. One result was *The Day in Bohemia, or Life Among the Artists* (1912), a remarkable tour de force that, even while making satirical asides, details in rhymed stanzas the bohemian life of Greenwich Village, which was the breeding ground of the original Beats. Reed's wordplay and spirit presaged Beat poetry: "Inglorious Miltons by the score, / Mute Wagners, Rembrandts, ten or more / And Rodins, one to every floor. / In short, those unknown men of genius who dwell in third-floor rears gangrenous, / Reft of their rightful heritage / By a commercial soulless age. / Unwept, I might add, and unsung, / Insolvent, but entirely young."[6]

Unlike many of his contemporaries, Reed had talent that reached beyond the close-knit bohemian circles. Prodded by an undying idealism and superhuman energy, he turned to journalism. By age 27 he was the country's top war correspondent, writing mostly for *The Masses*, an influential leftist magazine. He went to Russia to view the revolution, wrote a firsthand account (*Ten Days That Shook the World*), and died there in 1920. He is the only American ever buried in the Kremlin.

That same spirit of liberation was carried over the next three decades, when the Siren call of Paris attracted Americans like Gertrude Stein, Ernest Hemingway, Henry Miller, Anaïs Nin, and countless lesser-known writers and artists. By the early 1950s Manhattan's bohemian enclaves experienced a resurgence, with the abstract expressionist painters and other members of the city's avant-garde holding court at such Greenwich Village venues as the Cedar Tavern (82 University Place), the Minetta Tavern (Minetta Lane), and San Remo Café (at Bleecker and MacDougal). Among the San Remo's regulars were a veritable Who's Who of American arts and letters: James Agee, Maxwell Bodenheim, John Cage, Merce Cunningham, Miles Davis, Dorothy Day, Paul Goodman, Chester Kallman, Harold Norse, Larry Rivers, Gore Vidal, and virtually everybody associated with Judith Malina and Julian Beck's newly launched Living Theatre.

Kerouac and his friends were well aware and appreciative of these antecedents. They, in fact, often rubbed shoulders with Bodenheim and other legendary bohemians in and around Manhattan, like Alice Neel and Joe Gould. David Amram recalled how one night as he and Kerouac were strolling toward MacDougal and Bleecker Streets in the heart of Greenwich Village, when Kerouac turned to him and asked, "Can you see the ghosts of O. Henry, Edna St. Vincent Millay, and Eugene O'Neill hovering above us?" The fledgling Beats were also not so self-important as to possess a carefully thought-out "movement." Kerouac tried to, in hindsight, concoct some "rules" that would express the differences ("Beliefs & Technique for Modern Prose" and "Essentials of Spontaneous Prose") and then he and Holmes tried to "explain" the whole thing via mainstream venues like the *New York Times* and *Esquire*. Holmes, in particular, went the extra mile with his article "This Is the Beat Generation," published in the *New York Times Sunday Magazine* on November 16, 1952, soon after his first

> The first "Beat Generation" novel was not, as many believe, Jack Kerouac's *On the Road*. That honor belongs to *Go* by John Clellon Holmes, which depicted some of the same characters as Kerouac did but was published five years earlier, in 1952. Kerouac did write about a "beat generation" in his first novel, *The Town and the City*, published in 1950, but editors chose to remove the references.

novel, *Go*—which depicted the fledgling Beat Generation—was published. Holmes also published an essay called "The Philosophy of the Beat Generation" in the February 1958 issue of *Esquire*, an attempt by a mainstream periodical to explain the new counterculture to elders who "were completely flabbergasted." These were efforts to put a meaning on something that was still in flux, still unfolding as the initial circle of friends (Kerouac, Ginsberg, and Burroughs) expanded to embrace the whole world.

Indeed, it was not until the monumental 1957 publication of *On the Road* by Jack Kerouac that the "Beat Generation" existed as a media phenomenon. And the closest thing to a Beatnik manifesto was *On the Road* or Ginsberg's "Howl," both of which were published years after the events depicted therein took place. Both of these now classic works can and should be read as windows on a uniquely American counterculture.

Notes

1. Ann Charters, ed., *The Portable Beat Reader* (New York: Viking, 1992), xxxiv.
2. Steven Watson, *The Birth of the Beat Generation: Visionaries, Rebels, and Hipsters, 1944–1960* (New York: Pantheon, 1995), 3.
3. John Clellon Holmes, *Go* (New York: Thunder's Mouth, 1997), 36.
4. Jack Kerouac, *On the Road* (New York: Viking, 1957), 145–146.
5. Michael T. Kaufman, "At 78, Someone Who Is Still Beat Yet Undefeated." *New York Times*, December 9, 1992, B3.
6. John Reed, *The Day in Bohemia* (1912).

CHAPTER TWO

How the Beats Turned into Beatniks

To Kerouac's definition for the *Random House Dictionary* (see chapter 1) can be added many other characteristics of those who came to be known as "the Beats" and/or "Beatniks." To be a "Beatnik" was as much of an attitude and a style as it was an adherence to any literary or philosophical code of conduct or artistic theory. The Beat soundtrack would feature groundbreaking improvisational jazz by the likes of Charlie "Bird" Parker, Thelonious Monk, Dizzy Gillespie, and Miles Davis, and the art backdrop would be the large abstract-expressionist canvases by the likes of Franz Kline, Robert Motherwell, Larry Rivers, Jackson Pollock, Willem de Kooning, and Robert De Niro Sr. (yes, the actor's father). For drama, Julian Beck and Judith Malina's experimental Living Theatre set the standard, and for dance, Merce Cunningham was redefining performance art.

Although bongo drums have been associated—in cartoons, TV shows, movies, and joke books—with "Beatniks," these percussion instruments were not the staple of the early Beat Generation circle. Bongo drums derived from Cuban salsa music, which was certainly being played in Manhattan during the 1940s and 1950s. But bongos were never part of the standard bebop jazz lineup and only began appearing as a cultural fad, and because they were a relatively cheap way to entertain a crowd at a party or poetry reading. However, bongo drums are mentioned only once in Kerouac's own writings, in a true-to-life account of a concert by Bulee "Slim" Gaillard that can be found in *On the Road*, wherein he ("Sal") and Neal Cassady ("Dean") fall into a Beat reverie over the performer's exotic playing of the bongos:

> But one night we suddenly went mad together again; we went to see Slim Gaillard in a little Frisco nightclub. Slim Gaillard is a tall, thin Negro with big sad eyes who's always saying, "Right-orooni" and "How 'bout a little bourbonorooni." In Frisco great eager crowds of young semi-intellectuals sat at his feet and listened to him on the piano, guitar, and bongo drums. When he gets warmed up he takes off his shirt and undershirt and really goes. He does and says anything that comes into his head. He'll sing "Cement Mixer, Put-ti Put-ti" and suddenly slow down the beat and brood over his bongos with fingertips barely tapping the skin as everybody leans forward breathlessly to hear; you think he'll do this for a minute or so, but he goes right on, for as long as an hour, making an imperceptible little noise with the tips of his fingernails, smaller and smaller all the time till you can't hear it any more and sounds of traffic come in the open door. Then he slowly gets up and takes the mike and says, very slowly, "Great-orooni . . . fine-ovauti . . . hello-orooni . . . bourbon-orooni . . . all orooni . . . orooni . . . vauti . . . oroonirooni. . . ." He keeps this up for fifteen minutes, his voice getting softer and softer till you can't hear. His great sad eyes scan the audience.[1]

The improvisational spirit of bebop jazz was really what inspired the major Beat writers and artists. As writer James Campbell noted,

> Since the early 1950s, following the composition of *The Town and the City* and the first version of *On the Road*, Kerouac had moved his method of composition ever closer to the area of music. He "blew" on his typewriter as a jazz musician blew on his instrument. It wasn't cool jazz, it was bebop, hard and fast, the faster the better, until the melody was lost in a blur of notes. Kerouac could type faster than anyone else, according to Philip Whalen: "The most noise that you heard while he was typing was the carriage

return, slamming back again, and again. The little bell would bing-bang, bing-bang, bing-bang! And he'd laugh and say, 'Look at this!' And he'd type, and he'd laugh. Then he'd make a mistake, and this would lead him off into a possible part of a new paragraph, into a funny riff of some kind."[2]

Though the Beat Generation revered the more intellectual bebop jazz, with its emphasis on spontaneity, and not the popular new rock 'n' roll—dominated by a simple beat and a two-minute song format—young people still flocked to Kerouac's *On the Road* when it was published in 1957. As a result, the novelistic chronicle of his friends' peripatetic restlessness became more of a social phenomenon than a literary work and Kerouac became the unlikely (and often unwilling) spiritual leader for a huge amorphous army of followers. Thus, when he was dubbed "The King of the Beats," Kerouac was overwhelmed by the scrutiny that that implied.

While Kerouac, rightfully, was considered the literary force behind the Beat Generation, Holmes was the author of the first published "Beat" novel. His *Go* (1952) was the first to put the term "beat" in print. Few more clear portraits, outside of straight biographies of the participants, can rival the accuracy of Holmes's thinly veiled fictional account of the initial core of people in Manhattan who would comprise the Beat Generation. In the introduction to a 1976 reissue of his novel, Holmes noted,

> Very little in it is fictionalized. . . . I'm amazed now to see how slavishly it hews to real events and real people. Even whole conversations are verbatim. I had been keeping exhaustive work-journals for two previous years, and the book was more or less a transcription of these day-to-day jottings. In fact, the first draft was written with the real names intact, and several of the actual protagonists read it during its composition. The reader will have little trouble identifying the characters based on Jack Kerouac, Allen Ginsberg, Neal Cassady, Herbert Huncke and other writers and personalities associated with the Beat Generation.[3]

The novel is so similar to *On the Road*, at least in the events depicted, that some people later accused Holmes of copying Kerouac.

This was not true. He and Kerouac were close friends and literary confidants. Kerouac was well aware of Holmes's efforts to write *Go*, and even read early drafts of the manuscript and made editorial suggestions. He himself was simultaneously working on a novel that would cover some of the same territory, and Holmes advised him on that work, what would become *On the Road*, as well. Holmes noted, "Jack read *Go* over the two years during which I wrote it, two years during while he was unsuccessfully trying to get *On the Road* on the road, and it was after he finished reading my first draft in early March of 1951 that he began what would be the final, twenty-day version of his own book, completed in late April of that year." It would be six frustrating and peripatetic years before Kerouac would see his most famous book finally in print.[4]

> While writing and typing the manuscript of *On the Road*, Kerouac listened repeatedly to an album by jazz bandleader-drummer Max Roach. He incorporated Roach's "percussive emphasis" into his writing. Kerouac could accurately type 100 words per minute, a pace he was capable of sustaining for several consecutive days.

The protagonist of *Go*, Paul Hobbes (modeled on Holmes), is an intellectual whose life has fallen into an unchanging rut, until he befriends a group of people through his pal Gene Pasternak (modeled on Kerouac). These include David Stofsky (Allen Ginsberg) and Hart Kennedy (Neal Cassady). Holmes captured the essence of the people who would later be known as "Beatniks." Holmes wrote,

> Hobbes ventured into the outskirts of this world suspiciously, even fearfully, but unable to quell his immediate fascination for he had been among older, less active, and more mental people for too long, and needed something new and exciting. . . . He came to know their world, at first only indirectly. It was a world of dingy backstairs "pads," Times Square cafeterias, bebop joints, night-long wanderings, meetings on street corners, hitchhiking, a myriad of "hip" bars all over the city, and the streets themselves. It was inhabited by people "hungup" with drugs and other habits, searching out a new degree of craziness. . . . They kept going all the time, living by night, rushing

around to "make contact," suddenly disappearing into jail or on the road only to turn up again and search one another out. They had a view of life that was underground, mysterious, and they seemed unaware of anything outside the realities of deals, a pad to stay in, "digging the frantic jazz," and keeping everything going. . . . Once Pasternak said to him with peculiar clarity: "You know, everyone I know is kind of furtive, kind of beat. They all go along the street like they were guilty of something, but didn't believe in guilt. I can spot them immediately! And it's happening all over the country, to everyone; a sort of revolution of the soul, I guess *you'd* call it!"[5]

Further on, Hobbes's "effort to transcribe his feelings of discovery which somehow failed, and so he wrote on and on about 'this beat generation, this underground life!'"[6]

The most salient feature of the "Beat Generation," though, was that Kerouac and his fellow travelers—Cassady, Ginsberg, Burroughs, Corso, Snyder, and every other figure covered in this book—broke the rules. Further, they broke *all* of the rules—of writing, artistry, decorum, dress, talk, music, vices. The Beat Generation sought nothing less than a clean break from the past. That, in itself, was enough to condemn anyone associated with it in the eyes of an establishment flush from victory in World War II and staking out the moral and political high ground against world communism.

While the word "Beatnik" was intended as a pejorative when it was coined in 1958, it has endured in the American lexicon. Today, it no longer has negative connotations. Rather, "Beatnik" has come to embody the best aspects of the Beat Generation. To be "beat" is

---

Kerouac's first real "Beat" publication was "Jazz of the Beat Generation," an excerpt from his unpublished *On the Road* and *Visions of Cody* manuscripts. This amalgamation appeared in April 1955 in the paperback anthology *New World Writing*, under the byline "Jean-Louis." The biographical note reads, "This selection is from a novel-in-progress, *The Beat Generation*. Jean-Louis is the pseudonym of a young American writer of French-Canadian parentage. He is the author of one published novel." Kerouac was paid $106 for the piece.

tantamount today to being "punk." John Holmstrom, founder and editor of *Punk* magazine, told this author, "Of course, the Beats were a big influence on punk. . . . I remember when CBGBs hosted poetry readings, back when Patti Smith and Television were the biggest names. Also, Maynard G. Krebs [a Beatnik character in the popular TV show *The Many Loves of Dobie Gillis*] was a very important cultural influence on so many of us." To Holmstrom, Kerouac and the Beat Generation's careening into public consciousness in the 1950s was no different than the Ramones, Johnny Rotten, and the Sex Pistols doing the same thing in the 1970s. The Beats and punks can both be summed up by this often-quoted line from *On the Road*:

> Because the only people for me are the mad ones, the ones who are mad to live, mad to talk, mad to be saved, desirous of everything at the same time, the ones who never yawn or say a commonplace thing, but burn, burn, burn like fabulous yellow roman candles exploding like spiders across the stars.[7]

The front-jacket blurb on the first paperback edition of *On the Road* makes it clear that the book was the literary equivalent of a Marlon Brando or James Dean film: "This is the bible of the 'beat generation'—the explosive bestseller that tells all about today's wild youth and their frenetic search for Experience and Sensation." The back jacket blurb took it further: "Wild drives across America . . . buying cars, wrecking cars, stealing cars, dumping cars, picking up girls, making love, all-night drinking bouts, jazz joints, wild parties, hot spots. . . . This is the odyssey of the Beat Generation, the frenetic young men and their women restlessly racing from New York to San Francisco, from Mexico to New Orleans in a frantic search—for Kicks and Truth." *Time* magazine called it "A kind of literary James Dean."[8]

Kerouac's words—and even his two main characters' names (Sal Paradise and Dean Moriarty)—had the sound of prophecy in a time that, on the surface, valued conformity above all other things. "Paradise" is self-explanatory—a name that suggests a perfection of mind, body, and spirit. "Moriarty" is more subtle, echoing "Professor Moriarty" from Arthur Conan Doyle's Sherlock Holmes tales, the man who served as the archenemy of the great detective, and even the dark side of his own genius. Neal Cassady, on whom Dean Moriarty is

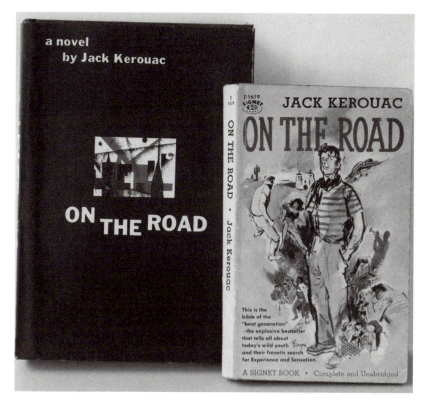

Jack Kerouac's novel On the Road *was the book that launched the Beat Generation. Many editions have been published since 1957, including the first hardcover edition (Viking Press) and the first paperback edition (Signet). (Courtesy of Tom Hearn.)*

based, played that role at times in Jack Kerouac's life, both goading him on and leaving him in the lurch. Kerouac coined a term for this two-sided coin that was Dean Moriarty: "The Holy Goof."

But why would such artists and characters want to rock the boat of post–World War II prosperity? Young people were set to explode. Beneath the surface of the complacent and conformist Eisenhower era was a hunger for change, driven by the urges and frustrations of the young. And, indeed, the Beat message spread like gospel among the young and restless, most of whom felt that Marlon Brando's character in *The Wild One* (1953) spoke directly to them when he responded to the question, "What are you rebelling against?"—while listening to jazz on the jukebox—"What've you got?"

Widening the Beat Circle

Though many historians have claimed that the members of the Beat Generation only consisted of a core of writers, such narrowness of scope does not take into account that this small group was itself shaped by the subterranean currents flowing through the New York scene. It also restricts the movement to purely a literary one, which is just plain factually wrong. The Beat Generation was not just a literary movement. It embraced music, art, dance, theater, photography, film, and even television. Like all distinct and distinctive subcultures before and since, the Beats fused their lives with their art, embraced the unconventional, and developed their own unique style and language. When asked, "What do you think about the Beat Generation?" Gregory Corso responded, "A certain style, when you look back on it, old photos, Fitzgerald in Paris, 1920, high society, prohibition, jazz; that's more what characterized a generation than what they believed in. The fundamental facts are always the same, the style changes, but the facts, my boy, the facts remain."[9]

Thus, widening the initial inner circle a bit, we find numerous shapers of subculture who influenced Kerouac, Ginsberg, Burroughs, and Cassady and those around them, including the mercurial Corso, as well as Herbert Huncke, John Clellon Holmes, Lucien Carr, and so on. Once the movement and its undercurrent of style spread nationwide, any number of seminal figures fell under the Beat Generation umbrella, in San Francisco, Los Angeles, Black Mountain, North Carolina, New York's Greenwich and East Villages, Near North Side in Chicago, New Orleans, and elsewhere; indeed, it seemed every large and diverse American city had a small pocket of Beatnik activity going on, in galleries, coffeeshops, bars, and city parks.

In one sense, the "Beat Generation" was not unlike a semantic vacuum cleaner, pulling all manner of rebellion together in one place. Even motorcycle rebels like Brando's character or leather-jacketed juvenile delinquent hot-rodders like James Dean's character in *Rebel Without a Cause* (1955) were pulled into the Beat Generation orbit, partly because the label gave the media something around which to weave narratives of youthful rebellion. Like the "hippie" banner of the 1960s, the term "Beat"—in the eyes of the mainstream media—came to include anything maladjusted, inarticulate, rebellious, lazy and/or delinquent. What had begun in the mid- to late 1940s in the bars, coffeeshops, nightclubs, and galleries of New York and on the high-ways between the East and West coasts as an earnest attempt to define a newly emerging underground spirit in America—with its attendant arts and letters and style and language—had turned into a

"Like help!"

A Beat Generation Joke Book *(Signet, 1959) was a satiric take on the Beatnik phenomenon, which included this cartoon about a drowning Beatnik. (Courtesy of Tom Hearn.)*

media stereotype by the late 1950s. That stereotype was of a babbling, bearded, beret-wearing "beatnik" whose every other word was "like." (A popular "beatnik humor" book of the time featured a cartoon beatnik who, while drowning, cries out, "Like help!")

The "Beatnik" was initially a derisive term coined in 1958 by *San Francisco Chronicle* columnist Herb Caen, meant to satirize the "weekend Beats" who had begun to flood the jazz clubs, coffeehouses, and art galleries that had sprung up, like mushrooms after a summer rain, in the wake of Kerouac's ascendancy in the North Beach area of the city. The word "Beatnik" derives from the Soviet satellite "*Sputnik,* which was launched in October 1957, further fueling Cold War tensions between the Soviet Union and the United States. Self-respecting Beats did not refer to themselves as Beatniks. On April 2, 1958, months after *Sputnik* was launched, Caen wrote, "*Look* Magazine, preparing a picture spread on San Francisco's Beat Generation (oh, no, not AGAIN!), hosted a party in a North Beach house for 50 Beatniks, and by the time word got around the sour grapevine, over 250 bearded cats and kits were on hand, slopping up Mike Cowles's free booze. They're only Beat, y'know, when it comes to work."[10]

Just as it had been when the hippies emerged as a viable counterculture in the 1960s, and the punks in the 1970s, the sure sign that a new day had dawned was that the old order rose up to renounce it. Jonathan Swift once spoke to this recurrent waxing and waning of what are now called the culture wars in *Thoughts on Various Subjects, Moral and Diverting.* Three centuries later, Swift's words still ring true: "When a true genius appears in the world, you may know him by this sign, that the dunces are all in confederacy against him."[11]

And, just as Swift prophesied, the critics came together to exhibit their loathing for the Beats, each trying to one-up the other for the sharpest rebuke or most insulting putdown. Right-wing critic Norman Podhoretz famously labeled the Beats "Know-Nothing Bohemians," and the reactionary *National Review* called Beat poetry "a combination of nausea and the stirrings of the urino-genital tract." Meanwhile, left-leaning publications like *Saturday Review* said the Beats engaged in "unwashed eccentricity" while Diana Trilling, the doyenne of the liberal *Partisan Review* set, called the Beats poets "miserable children trying desperately to manage."

Even erstwhile compatriots of the Beats broke camp and ran to the hills when their infamy was assured—though, more likely, theirs was envious carping when their popularity was equally secure. As Dennis McNally wrote, "[Critics] were . . . troubled by the knowledge that more and more copies of "Howl" and *On the Road* were going out to Des Moines and Pocatello and El Paso, where few people indeed bought the *Partisan Review*."[12] McNally might have easily added *Saturday Review, Commentary,* the *New Yorker, Kenyon Review, Hudson Review,* or any of the other preferred journals of literary sophisticates and culture snobs. Among those who had previously embraced the Beat currents but now rejected them were Kenneth Rexroth, a powerful literary figure in the San Francisco Bay Area, and Herbert Gold, a novelist and classmate of Kerouac's at Columbia. Gold envied Kerouac his success, sniping from the pages of *Playboy* that the Beats possessed little talent. Gold also, in a 1957 review of *On the Road* for *The Nation,* advised: "Hipster, Go Home."[13]

The most infamous of the putdowns came from Truman Capote, who in late 1959 took part in a panel discussion with Dorothy Parker (who disliked the Beat Generation) and Norman Mailer (who came to their defense) on David Susskind's *Open Forum* television program: "None of these people [in the Beat Generation] have anything interesting to say and none of them can write, not even Mr. Kerouac. . . . That isn't writing at all—that's typing."[14]

Jack Kerouac was an easy target at the time, simply because he was the biggest. His 1957 novel *On the Road* was nothing less than, wrote *New York Times* book reviewer Gilbert Millstein, a "historic occasion." Millstein hailed it as "an authentic work of art" and "a major novel," and he drew the line in the cultural sand by suggesting *On the Road* was "the most beautifully executed, the clearest and most important utterance yet made by the generation Kerouac himself named years ago as 'beat,' and whose principal avatar he is."

On the Road ushered in a paradigm shift in postwar American literature, as well as offering an entirely new way to look at, and live in, the world. This new "Beat" or beatnik mindset served as a viable alternative to the squeaky clean, ultraconservative, and conformist mainstream consumer culture of the 1950s.

> The lavish review of *On the Road* in the *New York Times* on September 4, 1957, was written by Gilbert Millstein, a music critic for the newspaper. The only reason Millstein reviewed *On the Road* was that the regular book reviewers were on vacation. He wrote, "Just as, more than any other novel of the Twenties, *The Sun Also Rises* came to be regarded as the testament of the Lost Generation, so it seems certain that *On the Road* will come to be known as that of the Beat Generation." Millstein called its publication "a historical occasion." His review launched Kerouac's career and, in turn, the rise of the Beat Generation.

Kerouac followed the notoriety brought to him by *On the Road* by trying to disappear into nature (*The Dharma Bums, Desolation Angels*), travel (*Lonesome Traveler, Mexico City Blues, Tristessa*), and alcohol (*The Subterraneans, Big Sur*). But the public still sought him out, and often found him—older, darker, more tattered than their fantasies of the "King of the Beats."

> The closing lines of Kerouac's *The Subterraneans* are: "And I go home having lost her love. And write this book." That is, literally, what he did. After his breakup with the woman who inspired the book, Alene Lee, he typed his novel in three days.

On the Road was not the only gauntlet tossed at the feet of the postwar American establishment. Allen Ginsberg's book-length poem "Howl" may have been even more wide-reaching. Certainly, it was more controversial than anything Kerouac wrote. But Ginsberg was also the most tireless champion and exemplar of all things Beat, and the most patient and effective at deflecting the criticism.

Kerouac wearied of having to justify or explain the behavior of "Beatniks." To clear the air, he wrote an essay called "The Origins of the Beat Generation" for *Playboy*, published in 1959. In it, Kerouac wrote,

> Woe, woe unto those who think that the Beat Generation means crime, delinquency, immorality, amorality . . . woe unto those who attack it on the grounds that they simply don't understand history

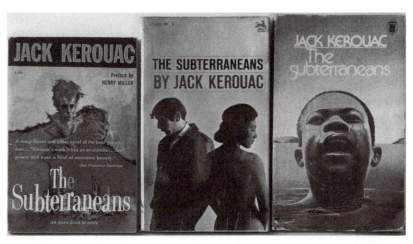

Jack Kerouac wrote The Subterraneans *in October 1953, in a sustained 72-hour burst of creation. Not published until 1958,* The Subterraneans *was based on his thwarted love affair with the part-Cherokee, part-black bohemian Alene Lee. It inspired a Hollywood film and has never been out of print, as these different editions attest. The first paperback edition, with Henry Miller's preface, is seen at left. (Courtesy of Tom Hearn.)*

and the yearnings of human souls . . . woe unto those who don't realize that America must, will, is, changing now, for the better I say . . . woe unto those who make evil movies about the Beat Generation where innocent housewives are raped by beatniks! . . . woe unto those who spit on the Beat Generation, the wind'll blow it back.[15]

> Kerouac's original title for *On the Road* was *The Beat Generation*. His original title for *The Dharma Bums* was *Avalokitevara*, which he described in a letter (dated May 31, 1957) to his agent Sterling Lord, as "a picaresque account of how I discovered Buddha and what happened in my experiences, often hilarious, as an American Dharma Bum (or bhikku, wandering religious teacher)."

The public perception of the Beatnik was of a person who was almost unapproachably cool and inscrutably intellectual. In *Desolation Angels* (written in 1961; not published until 1965), Kerouac expressed his regrets over how misused the term "beat" had become:

To think that I had so much to do with it, too, in fact that very moment the manuscript of *On the Road* was being linotyped for imminent publication and I was already sick of the whole subject. Nothing can be more dreary than coolness, postured, actually secretly rigid coolness that covers up the fact that the character is unable to convey anything of force or interest, a kind of sociological coolness soon to become a fad up into the mass of middle class youth.[16]

On the back cover of the original New American Library's 1959 edition of *The Dharma Bums* is written: "From the pagan depths of Frisco's bohemian bars to the dizzying heights of the snow-capped Sierras. . . . This is the story of two sensation-seeking hipsters and their jet-propelled search for Experience." The book's "sex orgies" and "marathon wine-drinking binges" are also highlighted.

Allen Ginsberg came to Kerouac's defense after a *New York Times* book critic slammed Kerouac's 1959 novel *Dr. Sax*. In a stinging letter to the editor, Ginsberg wrote, in part,

The foul word "beatnik" is used several times to describe either Kerouac or his characters. . . . Must this journalistic sneer continue to be directed at artists? It is shameful. Then well may Kerouac continue to be Beat in America, a lone creator, like Melville, among generations of stereotypes. His Art's a wonder. To be Beat this way is noble. But the "beatnik" of mad critics is a piece of their own ignoble poetry. And if "beatniks" and not illuminated Beat poets, overrun this country, they will have been created not by Kerouac, but by industries of mass communication which continue to brainwash Man and insult nobility where it occurs. Prophetically, Allen Ginsberg.[17]

Beat Style

At a November 1958 "debate" on the topic "Is There a Beat Generation?" Jack Kerouac told the Hunter College Playhouse audience,

"Now there are two types of beat hipsters—the Cool: bearded, sitting without moving in cafes, with their unfriendly girls dressed in black, who say nothing; and the Hot: crazy, talkative, mad, shining eyes, running from bar to bar only to be ignored by the cool subterraneans. I guess I'm still with the hot ones: When I walk into a club playing jazz, I still want to shout, 'Blow, man, blow!' "[18]

Perhaps unknowingly, Kerouac touched on many of the mores, fashions, and styles of the so-called Beatniks. Previously known as "hipsters," Beatniks were active, alert, manic, and looking for new experiences with the fervor of explorers. The bohemian scene that grew up around the Beats was not dominated, as the critics insisted, by a bunch of layabouts and slackers. Rather, the Beatniks showed, in cities across the country, how down-at-the-heels neighborhoods could be transformed into hip Meccas, with some imagination and energy, despite a lack of funds. Lawrence Lipton noted, "An unrentable store, with its show windows curtained or painted opaque, becomes a studio. A loft behind a lunchroom or over a liquor store becomes an ideal pad where you can keep your hifi going full volume at all hours of the night and no neighbors to complain."[19]

One aspect of all bohemian scenes, not just the Beatniks', is the professed rejection of traditional "straight" style, including music, art, housing, and fashion. However, as the nascent scene begins to attract larger audiences of devotees and curiosity seekers, that unique personal style becomes codified, almost uniform, thus mirroring "straight" society's obsession with conformity. And then the next unique style change was launched.

For example, Kerouac's choice of flannel shirts, floppy hats, pants, and banged-up workman's boots was not a studied affectation. It was a pragmatic solution to a decided lack of funds and an itinerant lifestyle. Kerouac himself was never stylish, never wore a beret, goatee (or any facial hair whatsoever), never smoked a cigarette with a long holder or wore sunglasses or leather jackets. But those who came in his wake began to mimic him so completely that it seemed an entire generation had turned into lumberjacks overnight. The same dynamic could be seen in the wake of Marlon Brando's and James Dean's on-screen popularity, when American teenagers began to sport black leather jackets and riders caps, loafers, white socks and tight blue jeans.

"Subterranean" was the term Ginsberg used to describe his Beat comrades. Kerouac expropriated it for *The Subterraneans*, in which he described them as "hip without being corny, they are intellectual as hell and know all about Pound without being pretentious or talking too much about it, they are very quiet, they are very Christlike."

David Amram recalled one occasion when he and Kerouac visited a café in Greenwich Village in 1959. Amram wrote,

We eased our way through to the back room of the Figaro. It was jammed with young people, many wearing black berets, all black clothes, the young men sporting dark glasses and goatees, some carrying what appeared to be recently purchased knapsacks. Most of the young men and women were carrying books, whose covers they displayed as they spoke to one another. There were copies of *On the Road*, a poetry anthology by Dylan Thomas, and books by Sartre and Camus. Most of the young women wore black fishnet stockings, black skirts, and tight-fitting black sweaters. Many of the young men carried brand new bongos, some with the price tags still dangling from the tuning keys. "It's like Catholic school," said Jack. "Everyone's in uniform. . . . We're like tourists in a museum about ourselves."[20]

Steven Watson noted that most Beatniks worked "straight jobs" and at night flocked to the bohemian enclaves in the cities where they lived. In the Bay Area, this meant flocking to The Place for "Blabbermouth Night" or the Coexistence Bagel Shop or the hungry i and Purple Onion to see Lenny Bruce or Mort Sahl do stand-up comedy. Kenneth Rexroth and Lawrence Ferlinghetti read their poetry at The Cellar to jazz accompaniment, beginning another Beatnik affectation that was later co-opted and ridiculed as goateed men in berets banging on bongos. Many Beatniks, wrote Watson, "developed a distinct sartorial style that included faded black pants with loose threads at the cuff, tee-shirts, baggy sweaters, peasant blouses and long hair."[21]

Other Beat-style affectations that have been documented by Watson and Lipton: The use of utility companies' discarded telephone wire spools for tables, Chianti bottles with candles for lamps, and car seats for sofas. According to Watson, the "symptoms of the hipster" were: listens to jazz; wears beret, goatee, formal wear ("padded shoulders, thirty-one-inch pegs, two and seven-eights inch brim on the hat, roll collar, dark glasses"), jeans, black turtleneck sweater; uses pot; drinks espresso; "does nothing"; "knows existentialism"; "drinks heavily"; "likes Lord Buckley." The symptoms of the male Beatnik included: wears goatees, berets, jeans, second-hand clothing, silver crucifix pendants, dark glasses; uses marijuana; plays bongo; digs expressionist paintings; "chants poetry to jazz back-up"; "verges on the sexually ambiguous"; wears "hair over the collar"; and "appreciates Method acting." For females: wears jeans, black leotards, "waxy eye make-up"; "Morticia-like complexion, svelte, drinks dark espresso, cooks with garlic, dates black jazz players."[22]

Lipton noted that by 1959 the Beatnik styles had begun to infiltrate Madison Avenue advertising agencies, newspaper and magazine staffs, press agents, and Hollywood studios. Wannabe Beatniks started "to sprout beards and go to work in elkskin shoes, the lap-over Indian moccasin kind that no beatnik could ever afford . . . The girls had to save their new beat look for the weekends when they could go the limit with a way-off-the-shoulder, studiedly careless but conspicuously expensive get-up." On his home turf of Los Angeles, Lipton noted that by 1959,

> Nearly everybody paints or plays some kind of musical instrument, if only bongo drums or the recorder. And everybody writes poetry. . . . Many a Venice West landlord has walked into an apartment just vacated by some beatnik, who left without giving notice or paying back rent, to find all the walls and sometimes even the floors and doors covered with abstract murals, making it unrentable to anybody else except perhaps another beatnik.[23]

The Word on the Street

In 1960, *Beat Coast East*, an "anthology of rebellion" published by Stanley Fisher, tried to define what "Beat" meant. Editor Fisher, a well-known abstract expressionist painter among New York's avant-garde, asked a number of "squalid squares and plastered saints" in

Greenwich Village what they thought "Beat" meant. The answers were as follows:

1. A formal desperation which became a rebellion against all political and literary forms.
2. A new concept instinctively arrived at—a personal attitude that isn't in our vocabulary.
3. Very tired people—tired of living before one has started living, not being corny . . . cool.
4. Beat in a measure, pseudo-measure, pseudo-bohemian, pseudo-idealist, pseudo-writing, pseudo-reaction, pseudo-pseudo.
5. The immediacy of feeling god. A lack of fear—believing in yourself unburdened by others, corruption, commerce.
6. Unleashed conformity.
7. Cease to exist, renounce—beg—Now you're free!
8. A high level of mentality and awareness of the IDEA and of poetry and a non-involvement with one's own awareness. In that way one can't get hung up!
9. Beatitudes and the nostalgia for the word.
10. Playing double or nothing with God.
11. Means nothing: a category of names out of the mainstream of primitive evocation, a passion reaction of drums.
12. Beat existed before it was defined.
13. A prison yard for filthy children who don't know what they're talking about.
14. An uncertain Neo-Nihilism that has helped fill a void, that refreshes life through achieving a permanent death rattle.
15. A limpid and exhausted jazz rhythm . . . a knocked out and dragged down, an anything goes–get with it beat.
16. A dominant down beat, mainly a complaint which attempts to change worlds by words.
17. Playing safe.
18. The history of Zen and narcissism on Madison Avenue.
19. Just Nowhere.
20. Criminal without a crime.[24]

As Fisher intended, this list showed that no one—including those who took part in it—could agree on a definition of the "Beat

Generation," or Beatniks. And by the time the dictionary cited in the opening of this book was published, Kerouac was "on the road" to the graveyard (he would die October 21, 1969), his sidekick Neal Cassady had died in 1968, and a new "Hippie Revolution" was in full flower, peaking at the Woodstock pop festival in July 1969. Kerouac himself had long before wearied of the whole discussion, telling John Clellon Holmes, in a letter dated April 13, 1958, "The whole beat generation is a pain in the ass after [age] 35. . . . Once we had to cope, you and me, with ignorance of the world in general, and now we're being attacked and misrepresented by the very people who were supposed to understand and HELP us in our fight to instill peace & tenderness in the world. Instead, all this malice."[25] To Allen Ginsberg in a letter dated June 18, 1959, Kerouac wrote, "I saw a snapshot of myself taken recently in which I could see with my own eyes what all this lionized manure has done to me; it's killing me rapidly. I have to escape or die, don't you see."[26]

Kerouac never really did escape the "Beat" mantle, or his own personal demons. Nonetheless, his and his kindred spirits' creative legacy has inspired generations of Americans who have embraced it in their wake.

To be Beat, then, or to be a Beatnik, is to be heroically outside the mainstream of contemporary society.

Notes

1. Jack Kerouac, *On the Road* (New York: Viking, 1957), 145–146.
2. James Campbell, *This Is the Beat Generation* (London: Secker and Warburg, 1999), 121.
3. John Clellon Holmes, *Go* (New York: Thunder's Mouth, 1997).
4. Ibid., xix–xx.
5. Ibid., 36.
6. Ibid., 126.
7. Kerouac, *On the Road*, 8.
8. Jack Kerouac, *On the Road* (New York: Signet, 1958), cover.
9. Gregory Corso, "Variations on a Generation," in *The Portable Beat Reader*, ed. Ann Charters (New York: Viking, 1992), 184.
10. Herb Caen, "It's News to Me," *San Francisco Chronicle*, April 2, 1958.
11. John Kennedy Toole, *A Confederacy of Dunces*, frontispiece.

12. Dennis McNally, *Desolate Angel: Jack Kerouac, the Beat Generation, and America* (New York: Random House, 1979), 258.

13. Herbert Gold, "Hip, Cool, Beat, Frantic," *The Nation*, November 16, 1957.

14. Gerald Clarke, *Capote: A Biography* (Cambridge, MA: Da Capo, 2005), 315.

15. Jack Kerouac, "The Origins of the Beat Generation," *Playboy*, June 1959.

16. Jack Kerouac, *Desolation Angels* (New York: Viking, 1965), 121.

17. Allen Ginsberg, letter to the *New York Times*, 1959.

18. Marc Schleifer, "The Beat Debated," *Village Voice*, November 19, 1958.

19. Lawrence Lipton, *The Holy Barbarians* (New York: Julian Messner, 1959), 15–17.

20. David Amram, *Collaborating with Kerouac* (New York: Thunder's Mouth Press, 2002), 67–68.

21. Steven Watson, *The Birth of the Beat Generation: Visionaries, Rebels, and Hipsters, 1944–1960* (New York: Pantheon, 1995), 229.

22. Ibid., 259.

23. Lipton, *Holy Barbarians*, 255.

24. Stanley Fisher, *Beat Coast East: An Anthology of Rebellion* (New York: Excelsior, 1960), 7–8.

25. Jack Kerouac, *Selected Letters, 1957–1969*, ed. Ann Charters (New York: Viking, 1999), 121.

26. Ibid., 209.

CHAPTER THREE

The Emergence
of a Beatnik Voice

By 1954, Ginsberg had settled in the San Francisco Bay Area. He took a job as an advertising copywriter, met his lifelong companion Peter Orlovsky, and worked furiously on a long poem with a new style of long flowing lines and the cadences of an Old Testament prophet. On October 13, 1955, at the Six Gallery near the city's Embarcadero, Ginsberg unveiled this epochal work to the public. Partly because Ginsberg had done a great deal of advance publicity himself, the event turned into a cultural milestone. Biographer Ann Charters wrote, "It looked like the reading had called out the entire bohemian community of San Francisco, Marin County and the East Bay. There were left-over gypsies from the Stalinist era, Quaker-pacifists from World War II, all post-war alienated people, gradually discovering they had friends in the Bay Area."[1]

While all of the poets who participated in the Six Gallery reading (Michael McClure, Gary Snyder, Philip Lamantia, Philip Whalen, Lew Welch, and Allen Ginsberg) and the emcee, Kenneth Rexroth, were given appreciative receptions, it was Ginsberg's reading of excerpts from "Howl" that turned the event into something larger and more memorable than just a high-spirited evening. Kerouac, who had been invited to read but declined, secured several jugs of California wine, which he pressed on the 100 to 150 people squeezed into the tiny gallery. Kerouac—still relatively unknown in 1955—spent the evening sitting on the stage with a bottle of wine shouting, "Go! Go! Go!" (as he wrote in his depiction of the occasion in his 1958 novel *The Dharma Bums*). Rexroth told Ginsberg, "This poem will make you famous from bridge to bridge," meaning from the Golden Gate Bridge to the Brooklyn Bridge. And, indeed, he was right.[2]

Likewise, Ferlinghetti sent Ginsberg a telegram from San Francisco to his Berkeley cottage that read—in imitation of Ralph Waldo Emerson's letter to Henry David Thoreau—"I greet you at the beginning of a great career. When do I get the manuscript?" Ferlinghetti had used his City Lights Books as the base of a publishing imprint. He had begun publishing inexpensive "pocket book" editions (4 inches by 5 inches, priced 75 cents) of poetry, using for his model the small editions known as *Livres de poche* that he had bought while studying at the Sorbonne in Paris after serving in the U.S. Navy during World War II. The first in the series was his own small collection called *Pictures of a Gone World*, which contained some of the best of the early Beat poetry, including "The world is a beautiful place." Number 2 in the series was Kenneth Rexroth's *Thirty Spanish Poems of Love and Exile* and number 3 was Kenneth Patchen's *Poems of Humor and Protest*. Ginsberg's *Howl and Other Poems* was slated to be number 4.

Over the next few months, Ferlinghetti helped Ginsberg winnow through his manuscripts to pick the poems that would accompany "Howl" in the volume. They also found a way to organize the sprawling title poem, breaking it into three parts and including, as a separate poem, "A Footnote to Howl." The venerable poet William Carlos Williams agreed to write a short introduction to the volume, a major literary coup that grounded Beat poetry in the more "respectable" world of letters. Williams wrote, "Poets are damned but they are not

---

Kerouac suggested the title to Ginsberg's best-known poem, "Howl." In the dedication to his book *Howl and Other Poems*, Ginsberg wrote, "Several phrases and the title of 'Howl' are taken from [Jack Kerouac]."

blind, they see with the eyes of the angels. This poet sees through and all around the horrors he partakes of in the very intimate details of his poem. He avoids nothing, but experiences it to the hilt. . . . Hold back the edges of your gowns, Ladies, we are going through hell."[3]

Howl and Other Poems was published in September 1956 and quickly sold out in the Bay Area from word of mouth alone. As Ginsberg took his "act" on the road, to Los Angeles and New York, demand for the volume increased. Ferlinghetti quickly ran off a second printing. Because the books were printed in England and had to be shipped to America, City Lights just as quickly ran afoul of the law. Their second printing of *Howl and Other Poems* became a landmark work in the history of censorship in America.

As the notoriety of the poem spread, it had come to the attention of Chester MacPhee, collector of customs in San Francisco. After reading some of the descriptions of sex, drunkenness, and insanity, MacPhee claimed, "The words and the sense of the writing is obscene," and sought to ban the book. Because it had been printed in England, *Howl and Other Poems* had to pass through U.S. Customs to be legally sold in the United States. On March 25, 1957, customs agents seized 520 copies of the second printing as well as copies of a magazine called *The Miscellaneous Man*, both sold at City Lights Books; proprietors Ferlinghetti and Shigeyoshi Murao were arrested and jailed. The case went to trial when the ACLU contested the legality of the seizure; Ferlinghetti defended it on the grounds of literary merit, telling reporters, "I consider 'Howl' to be the most significant long poem to be published in this country since World War II, perhaps since Eliot's *Four Quartets*." Also coming to the defense of "Howl" were, to paraphrase the poem's now famous opening line, "the best minds of [Ginsberg's] generation." The prosecution called only two witnesses, one of whom suffered from the delusion that she had "rewritten Goethe's *Faust*." Had the judge ruled against *Howl and Other Poems*, and upheld the ban, the police department's Juvenile Bureau had prepared a list of other books it would ban, using Ginsberg's case as a precedent. Thus, in what was a resounding victory, Judge Clayton Horn ruled that the ban violated Ginsberg's First and Fourteenth Amendment rights, as well as the Constitution of the State of California, which says "Every citizen may freely speak, write, and publish his sentiments on all subjects, being responsible for the

Allen Ginsberg wrote *Kaddish*, his acclaimed book-length homage to his mother, Naomi, in a 30-hour session at the typewriter. He had been up all night at a friend's place and on his walk home he got the idea and cadence for the poem, which opens, "Downtown Manhattan, clear winter noon, and I've been up all night, talking, talking reading the Kaddish aloud, listening to Ray Charles blues shout blind on the phonograph . . ."

abuse of that right; and no law shall be passed to restrain or abridge the liberty of speech or of the press." The judge also cited the "motto" in Latin *"Honi soit qui mal y pense"* (Evil to him who evil thinks). City Lights Books was busted ten years later for selling Lenore Kandel's 1966 collection of erotic verse, *The Love Book*. A clerk at the Psychedelic Shop in Haight-Ashbury was arrested for the same offense. After a protest and staged reading of the offending passages by San Francisco State College professors, the charges were dropped.[4]

Beatnik poetry was deeply influenced by the patois of jazz musicians, as well as the improvisational aspects of bebop pioneers like Charlie Parker and John Coltrane. (As Kerouac advised writers, in his "Belief & Technique of Modern Prose," to "Blow as deep as you want to blow . . . the unspeakable visions of the individual. . . .") The mannerisms and iconoclasm of stand-up comics also influenced Beatnik poetry, especially those performers who walked and talked the Beat.

Among these were Lenny Bruce (born Leonard Schneider, 1925–1966). Bruce honed his comedic skills in the seedier clubs of Los Angeles, often accompanied by his wife, a stripper known as Honey Harlowe. After gaining a reputation among the hipster circles, he was invited to play jazz clubs where he opened for musicians like Woody Herman. Championed by influential Bay Area critic Ralph J. Gleason and Beat impresario Lawrence Ferlinghetti, Bruce was booked at San Francisco clubs where, by 1959, he was a favorite of the Beatnik crowds that poured into the city on weekends. His hip delivery, satiric takes on American culture, and boundary-pushing themes of race, religion, drugs, and sex created a furor, leading to his famous 1961 gig at Carnegie Hall in New York, as well as equally infamous busts on drug and obscenity charges. The mainstream media dubbed Bruce a "sick comic," with *Time* magazine riffing on the Beatnik connection, calling him "the most successful of the newer sickniks." Bruce further cemented his reputation with a freewheeling autobiography, *How to Talk Dirty and Influence People* (1963). By 1964 his performing career was stymied by obscenity busts, legal fees, and his own heroin addiction. Allen Ginsberg circulated a petition to give Bruce a fair hearing, which was signed by fellow Beats Lawrence Ferlinghetti, Gregory Corso, David Amram, and folksinger Bob Dylan. Bruce died from an overdose on August 3, 1966.

Another deeply influential hip comic was Mort Sahl (born 1927). Sahl traveled in the same Los Angeles and San Francisco circles as Lenny Bruce and, like Bruce, Sahl made people laugh and think simultaneously. Though they played the same clubs (the hungry i and Purple Onion in San Francisco, jazz clubs in Chicago and New York), Sahl was much more of a serious social and political commentator than Bruce. His routine was the personification of the hip intellectual. He claimed no political ideology (e.g., "I'm not a liberal, I'm a radical!"), and his blunt commentary contrasted starkly with the conformity of his times, making him popular among college students. In his memoir *Heartland*, Sahl wrote about his campus tours, "I thought it was important to tell young people that everyone twice their age is not corrupt."[5] Sahl dressed casually, usually in a V-neck sweater, and walked on stage with a rolled up newspaper in his hand. He then created a routine from that day's news items that not only informed his audience but forced them to rethink their own opinions (or, conversely, hardened the ones they had). He was one of the first comics to release record albums, including the popular *The Future Lies Ahead—Mort Sahl, Iconoclast* (1958), recorded at the hungry i. Sahl was popular on television and radio, too (unlike Bruce, he did not use obscenities); his was a voice of rebellion at a time when such things were rare on the airwaves. In the 1960s Sahl became obsessed with the assassinations of John and Robert Kennedy—to the detriment of his comedy, said the critics. Nonetheless, he influenced both George Carlin and Woody Allen (who likened Sahl's influence on comedy to that of Charlie Parker on jazz), as well as Chris Rock.[6]

The most influential of all, in the long run, may have been Lord Buckley, born Richard Myrtle Buckley (1906–1960). Lord Buckley was part stand-up comic and part conceptual artist whose stage routines consisted of monologues delivered in a hip lingo that was influenced by jazz but was partly self-invented. Buckley utilized various vocal styles that segued from a Southern "cracker" voice to that of a black jazz musician to a British lord to nonsense syllables and sound effects; he referred to his style as "hipsemantic." Born dirt poor to parents with some Native American blood, Buckley learned to hustle for work as everything from a truck driver to a lumberjack. He honed his performance skills in the speakeasies of Chicago in the late 1920s and on traveling vaudeville and medicine shows of the 1930s, then entertained American troops during World War II as part of the same USO tours that featured Bob Hope and Betty Grable. By the heyday of the Beatniks, Buckley had inhabited his alter ego as a British "lord" (he called his wife "Lady Buckley") and begun to play in jazz clubs in and around Los Angeles, where he caught the eyes, ears, and imaginations of budding Beatniks. Musician David Amram, who was friends with both Buckley and Jack Kerouac, said that Kerouac could "quote the comic's routines from memory."[7] Beat poet Lawrence Ferlinghetti also has acknowledged Buckley's influence on his poetry. Ferlinghetti even published, on his City Lights imprint, a book of Buckley's stage routines, *Hiperama of the Classics* (1960). Buckley released popular recordings, like "The Nazz" (a hip but non-blasphemous retelling of the life of Jesus of Nazareth) and "The Hip Ghan" (about Mahatma Gandhi). He also recited his own version of the Gettysburg Address (which opened "Four big hits and seven licks ago, our before-daddies swung forth upon this sweet groovy land a jumpin', wailin', stompin', swingin' new nation, hip to the cool sweet groove of liberty and solid sent upon the Ace lick dat all cats and kiddies, red, white, or blue, is created level in front . . ."). Buckley had his unique way of dressing (formal attire on stage, nude at home) and his own "look" (including his distinctive handlebar moustache).

Another of the thinking-person's favorite standup comics, Professor Irwin Corey (born 1914) claimed to be "The World's Foremost Authority." He was, in fact, not a professor, but a Brooklyn-born orphan who was once a featherweight boxing champion and union organizer. He created this alter ego by wearing formal attire, a stringy bow tie, wild Einstein-like hair and sneakers. Corey, like Buckley, would expostulate on any given subject, tying language in knots with academic jargon that sounded authentic but which made absolutely no sense. His hobo-professor shtick appealed to college students and

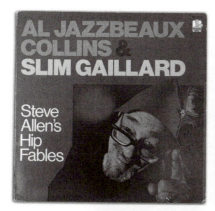

Though they dressed in black and feigned world-weariness, Beatniks enjoyed the idiosyncratic humor of Lord Buckley, Slim Gaillard, and Steve Allen, as well as the blistering stand-up comic routines of Lenny Bruce, whose humor was labeled "sick" by the mainstream press. (Courtesy of Tom Hearn.)

Beatniks, who admired Corey's ability to improvise under the stage lights. He honed his professor character at the same hip North Beach club where Sahl and Bruce played: the hungry i. Beneath the buffoonery was a more serious message. One of his signature routines, in fact, was to claim he'd gotten a copy of the Declaration of Independence from the federal government through a Freedom of Information Act request. Then he would pull out a mangled document with nearly every word blacked out. In 2008, at age 93, Corey was asked by a *New York Times* reporter for the meaning of life. His answer, "One of the things that you've got to understand is that we've got to develop a continuity in order to relate to exacerbate those whose curiosity has not been defended, yet the information given can no longer be used as allegoric because the defendant does not use the evidence which can be substantiated by," he said before finally asking, "What was the question?"[8]

Bulee "Slim" Gaillard (1916–1991) was a singer, pianist, and guitarist noted for his manic stage presence and unpredictable wordplay. His early recordings, as part of the jazz duo Slim and Slam, influenced young Jack Kerouac in the 1940s, especially the hits "Flat Foot Floogie (with a Floy Floy)," "Cement Mixer (Puti Puti)," and "The Groove Juice Special (Opera in Vout)." Other early jazz singers had a similar scat style, like Cab Calloway and Louis Jordan, but they could not improvise like Gaillard. Kerouac and his fellow Beats saw Gaillard perform often at Birdland, with Charlie Parker's and Coleman Hawkins's bands. Gaillard was immortalized by Kerouac in *On the Road*, when the narrator Sal Paradise and his friend Dean Moriarty wandered into a Gaillard performance. The pair were so smitten with Gaillard that they made a point of trying to meet him. This description is from *On the Road*:

> Dean stands in the back, saying "God! Yes!"—and clasping his hands in prayer and sweating. "Sal, Slim knows time, he knows time." . . . Now Dean approached him, he approached his God; he thought Slim was God; he shuffled and bowed in front of him and asked him to join us. "Right-orooni," says Slim; he'll join anybody but he won't guarantee to be there with you in spirit. Dean got a table, bought drinks, and sat stiffly in front of Slim. Slim dreamed over his head. Every time Slim said, "Orooni," Dean said, "Yes!" I sat there with these two madmen. Nothing happened. To Slim Gaillard the whole world was just one big orooni.[9]

Though he was best known as a TV host, comedian, and author, Steve Allen (1921–2000) was also an accomplished musician. After seeing Jack Kerouac read on stage at New York's Village Vanguard in late 1958, he convinced the camera-shy Kerouac to not only appear on his TV show in November 1959, but to allow Allen to improvise on the piano while Kerouac read. The result was so effective that the two men entered a recording studio soon thereafter and cut the best recordings of Kerouac reading.

Notes

1. Ann Charters, *Kerouac: A Biography* (New York: Warner Books, 1974), 240.
2. Barry Silesky, *Ferlinghetti: The Artist in His Time* (New York: Warner Books, 1990), 65.
3. Ibid., 67.
4. Alan Bisbort, *Media Scandals* (Westport, CT: Greenwood Press, 2008), 72–73.
5. Mort Sahl, *Heartland* (New York: Harcourt Brace Jovanovich, 1976), 75.
6. Woody Allen, *Woody Allen on Woody Allen: In Conversation with Stig Björkman* (New York: Grove Press, 1995), 30–31.
7. Don Waller, "Hipsters, Flipsters, and Skin-Poppin' Daddies," in *The Rolling Stone Book of the Beats: The Beat Generation and American Culture*, ed. Holly George-Warren (New York: Hyperion, 1999), 307.
8. Corey Kilgannon, "A Distinguished Professor with a Ph.D. in Nonsense," *New York Times*, April 14, 2008.
9. Jack Kerouac, *On the Road* (New York: Viking, 1957), 145–146.

| Beatniks Take
Manhattan,
the Nation, and
the World

The undercurrent of cultural change in America was in place long
before Jack Kerouac's *On the Road* and Allen Ginsberg's "Howl" gave
a new generation permission to crash the artistic barricades. Kindred
spirits were already gathering in bohemian enclaves around the country to express themselves or gather together around free-form poetry,
jazz (bebop), art (surrealism, abstract expressionism), photography
(WPA photographers, Robert Frank, Walker Evans), cinema (European "art" films, cinema verité, film noir), philosophy (existentialism,
Eastern), dance (modern, interpretive), and drama ("Theatre of the
Absurd" plays by Samuel Beckett, Albert Camus, Eugene Ionesco,
Jean Genet). A gay subculture also existed in postwar America, but
was so far in the closet that, unless one knew where to find it,
homosexuality as a lifestyle went undetected and gays adopted coded
language when making any references to it in "straight" society. One
could also find fakes, phonies, tourists, and hangers-on in the same
places one could find bohemian and Beatnik culture. This, of course,
could be said of any countercultural movement, especially in a consumer culture driven as it is by fads and trends.

Well-Known Beatnik Enclaves

New York City

The Beatnik may have been "named" in San Francisco (by *Chronicle* columnist Herb Caen), but he/she was born in New York City. This was the earliest stomping grounds of the group of kindred spirits who made up the Beat Generation, including Jack Kerouac, Allen Ginsberg, William Burroughs, Gregory Corso, Lucien Carr, John Clellon Holmes, and others. Their favorite haunts were found in three areas of Manhattan.

East Village/Greenwich Village: Cedar Tavern (82 University Place); San Remo Café (Bleeker and MacDougal); West 4th Bookstore, The Pony Stable (West 4th Street); the Gaslight (116 MacDougal). Of these, the San Remo was the most popular. According to Barry Miles, the San Remo was "the center of the bohemian life of Greenwich Village throughout the late forties and early fifties. To this crowd, Allen brought his friends Jack Kerouac, Carl Solomon, Lucien Carr, John Clellon Holmes, Philip Lamantia, Bill Cannastra. Alan Ansen, Joan Haverty, and William Burroughs. And the cross-pollination of various hip scenes occurred apace."

Fred McDarrah, tireless photographer and scene maker, included all of the following places near the intersection of Bleecker and MacDougal streets in Greenwich Village as Beat venues: Cock-n-Bull Café Theatre (149 Bleecker); Café Boria (186 Bleecker); Café Continental (111 MacDougal); The Figaro (185 Bleecker); Café Rafio (165 Bleecker); Playhouse Café (131 MacDougal); Café Rienzi (107 MacDougal); Café Wha? (115 MacDougal); Café Flamingo (178 Bleecker); The Gaslight (116 MacDougal); Dragon's Den (175 Bleecker); Take Three Café (149 Bleecker); The Bitter End (147 Bleecker); The Caricature (116 MacDougal); Café Bizarre (106 West 3rd Street); The Fat Black Pussycat (13 Minetta Lane).[1] Finally, Washington Square Park was a magnet for the entire Village, where Beat poets, dancers, musicians, artists, and chess players gathered.

Allen Ginsberg, in a 1946 journal entry, listed these as the Beats' favorite bars: Minetta's, George's, Beggar's. "Queer bars": Main Street Bar, MacDougals, Astor Men's Bar, Cerudi's, Jimmy's at 43rd, Tony Pastor's. For "jazz bars," Ginsberg listed the White Rose, the Village Vanguard, George's, Downbeat.

Harlem and Morningside Heights: On the Upper West Side near Columbia University, which Kerouac, Ginsberg, Carr, and Hal Chase attended. The West End (on Broadway, near West 114th Street) was the bar and restaurant where Kerouac met Lucien Carr who, in turn, introduced him to Allen Ginsberg and William Burroughs. It became a regular haunt of all the New York Beats throughout the late 1940s and 1950s.[2] In the 1960s, Columbia's radical students gathered here. Today, the West End is owned by a Columbia graduate who instituted an in-house brew called "Ker O'Whack" beer.

Midtown Manhattan: 52nd Street Jazz Club, the Angle Bar (8th Avenue and 42nd Street). The 42nd Street/Times Square area in general was a favorite haunt of the Beats, for its squalid and rough-hewn feel. This is where the Beats made the acquaintance of Herbert Huncke and his gang of thieves and hustlers.

San Francisco Bay Area

San Francisco was at the epicenter of a countercultural revolt that began long before the 1950s. Waves of nineteenth-century free spirits washed ashore in the Bay Area, including Samuel Clemens (aka Mark Twain), Ambrose Bierce, Bret Harte, Joachim Miller, George Sterling, Mary Austin and Gelett Burgess. The founder and driving force behind the irreverent literary magazine *The Lark*, Burgess (1866–1951) would become famous for absurd verse like "The Purple Cow" and his satiric "Map of Bohemia," which in 1896 contained such geographical features as "The Philistine Desert," "Vagabondia," and "Licentia." The Bay Area was also home to the originators of "road" literature upon which Kerouac would build his own legend: Jack London and John Muir. After the devastation of the 1906 San Francisco earthquake and fire, bohemians reappeared down the coast in Carmel and the Monterey Peninsula, which inspired the novels of John Steinbeck and William Saroyan, as well as the verse of Robinson Jeffers, a poet whose epic nature poetry wielded an influence on Beat writers like Gary Snyder and Michael McClure as well as on modern environmentalism.

The literary and arts scenes were already thriving in the Bay Area before Allen Ginsberg arrived in 1955 and Jack Kerouac and Neal and Carolyn Cassady settled here. By the late 1940s, the Bay Area had attracted an eclectic assortment of creative people and, more important, a ready audience for their works. In 1955 Lawrence Ferlinghetti became sole proprietor of City Lights Books, at 261 Columbus Avenue in North Beach, and began his own publishing imprint. Informal circles of writers and artists gathered at the area's small galleries, coffeehouses, and pubs. More formally, Ruth Witt-Diamant, who founded the Poetry Center at San Francisco State College in 1954, organized regular readings, lectures, and seminars with some of the world's most important writers, including W. H. Auden, Randall Jarrell, Louise Bogan, William Carlos Williams (who would champion Ginsberg), Malcolm Cowley (who would champion Kerouac), and even some of the young would-be Beats, like poets Michael McClure and Robert Creeley.

Also, on a weekly basis starting in the early 1950s, poet and translator Kenneth Rexroth held literary gatherings in his apartment at 250 Scott Street in San Francisco's Fillmore district. He had created a fertile environment for boundary-breaking literature. Every Wednesday, in 1957, he and Ferlinghetti performed poetry to jazz accompaniment at the Cellar (576 Green Street). In this same pre-Beat wave came poets Kenneth Patchen, Robert Duncan, Philip Lamantia, Jack Spicer, William Everson, and Josephine Miles (poet-in-residence at the University of California in Berkeley), artist Jean Varda, composer Harry Partch, writers Weldon Kees, Vincent McHugh, Henry Miller and Anaïs Nin. A visit by Dylan Thomas in 1952 was a seminal event in the San Francisco "poetry renaissance." Arguably the most famous poet in the world at the time, Thomas gave readings to packed Bay Area venues as well as on KPFA, a popular radio station. As Ferlinghetti noted, "His voice had a singular beauty and richness, in the great Welsh oral tradition; and the excitement he generated was an early inspiration for a tradition of oral poetry here, the subsequent San Francisco poetry movement (from the mid 1950s to the present) being consistently centered on the performance of poetry in public."[3]

One former Beatnik recalled, on the Web site Mudcat Café, how

> I would go up to North Beach to the bars that had been famous hang-outs for the Beats: often Vesuvio, a perfect bar for tourists, and the Coffee Gallery, which at that time catered to the young folk-music crowd and to young wannabe Beatniks who

might play chess at the table in the front window. On Friday and Saturday nights, the two blocks of Grant Avenue from Vallejo Street to Union Street would be completely filled with people. The crowd would yield only slowly and reluctantly for the occasional car that tried to come through, honking its horn. Lots of Gray Line tour busses came and didn't mind the fact that progress up these two blocks took forever. We "beatniks" were what the tourists had come to see, and the slower the bus went, the better look they got. Meanwhile, we made faces at the spectators and beat on the sides of the bus with our hands, confirming the belief of the tourists that we were very dangerous beatniks. It was a great show. I hope that Gray Line charged a whole lot for it. Around the corner from the Coffee Gallery, on Green Street, was a much more rau- cous bar: the Anxious Asp. . . . There was one homely looking girl in the crowds on Grant Avenue and in the Anxious Asp that I especially noticed. She used to sing blues sometimes at the Coffee Gallery, especially on Sunday evenings when they had the "hoote- nanny" (i.e., open mike), and she had a very loud voice that I liked a whole lot. But despite her singing ability, she didn't seem to be able to find acceptance. I would look at her and think, "There's someone who's even more lost in this scene than I am." A few years later, when I would frequently see her face in newspapers and mag- azines, I found out that it was Janis Joplin.[4]

According to *The Beat Generation Map of America*, the Beatnik hangouts in North Beach were Specs Bar (12 Adler Alley); Co- existence Bagel Shop (1398 Grant Street); The Place (1546 Grant Street), which was favored by artists and alumni of Black Mountain College and featured a weekly "Blabbermouth Night"; The Coffee Gallery (1353 Grant Street), run by Enrico Banducci who served an "Orgy of Poetry: Beat poets, neo-classic poets, strange poets, jazz poets, white rabbit poets, metaphysical poets"; Caffe Trieste (606 Val- lejo); The Cellar (576 Green Street), where Ferlinghetti and Kenneth Patchen read to jazz accompaniment and Lenny Bruce performed; Sam Wo's (813 Washington Street); and Vesuvio's (255 Columbus Street).[5] Steven Watson, in his detailed tapestry of San Francisco "Bohemias," called the Black Cat Café (710 Montgomery Street) "the reigning hangout of San Francisco bohemia for at least a decade."

He also cited Foster's Cafeteria (235 Montgomery Street), where Ginsberg and Orlovsky "exchanged vows"; the hungry i (599 Jackson Street), where standup comics Lenny Bruce and Mort Sahl held court and where the Beat opera "The Pizza Pusher" was performed; and City Lights (261 Columbus Avenue). Beat hotels included Cameo Hotel (389 Third Street), where Kerouac wrote "San Francisco Blues"; Hotel Wentley (1214 Polk Street), where Ginsberg met Orlovsky in Robert LaVigne's room; and the San Francisco State Poetry Center (1600 Holloway Avenue), founded by Ruth Witt-Diamant. Also influential were the art galleries and avant-garde theatre groups of note in the area: San Francisco Mime Troupe, the Committee, the Diggers. Likewise, nightspots of note: Purple Onion, Longshoreman's Hall, the Matrix, Blue Unicorn, Coffee and Confusion, Vesuvios, Keystone Korner, Robbies, Steppenwolf, No Name Pub, as well as many other unnamed spots taken over briefly by kindred spirits.[6]

After the Beats created their own mayhem here, the free spirit continued unabated into the 1960s. Various pockets, cliques, and enclaves of greater or lesser artistic, spiritual, political, racial, intellectual, mental, emotional, culinary, and chemical ferment could be found, like spores shot from a magic seedpod, throughout the Bay Area: Berkeley, Sausalito, Mill Valley, Bolinas, Point Reyes, Mount Tamalpais, Oakland, Santa Cruz, Big Sur, Carmel, Monterey. Within the city limits of San Francisco itself, there were even smaller though no less fertile seedlings, each with their own legacy of artistic, spiritual, and historic ferment: North Beach, Russian Hill, Chinatown, Jackson Square, Portsmouth Square, Union Square, Telegraph Hill, the Mission District, Fillmore, and, later, Haight-Ashbury. Even while the latter became the best known of these during the 1960s, it was, in many ways, the last gasp of an evolutionary process, the final straw that stirred the countercultural drink, the black hole that absorbed all the disparate waves of all these other enclaves. And the Beats continue to go on in San Francisco to this day.

Palo Alto, California

Along the southernmost point of San Francisco Bay, in Palo Alto, Stanford University attracted a circle of writers and iconoclasts, many of whom lived on or near Perry Lane, including novelists Ken Kesey and Robert Stone. Kesey and Stone had both attended Stanford's acclaimed creative writing program and studied under Wallace Stegner. In 1959 Kesey volunteered to take part in a CIA-financed drug study at the nearby Menlo Park Veterans Hospital. He was dosed with LSD, psilocybin, mescaline, cocaine, AMT, and DMT, and wrote accounts of their effects. These experiences, in part, inspired his groundbreaking novel *One Flew Over the Cuckoo's Nest* (1962). Stone wrote about his Beat days in his memoir *Prime Green* (2007). Jerry Garcia was from the Palo Alto area and he met Phil Lesh, the Grateful Dead's bassist, at a party on Perry Lane.

Los Angeles and Venice Beach

Venice Beach, located just south of the more storied beach town of Santa Monica, was where the largest concentration of bohemians gathered in the Los Angeles area. Locals referred to it as "Venice West" and it was perhaps born to play this offbeat role. Venice began as the dream of a man named Abbot Kinney, who made his millions back East in tobacco and spent them purchasing 160 acres of marsh south of Santa Monica in 1900. He felt that his property evoked Venice, Italy, and he hired two architects to design a city accordingly, with streets, hotels, and 15 miles of cement-bottomed canals. By 1905 his canals were filled with water. Needing people to live in his faux Venice, Kinney hit upon the gimmick of gondolas, importing two dozen of Italy's finest gondoliers and bidding them to serenade prospective buyers. He also persuaded local merchants to build their businesses in Venetian Renaissance style. He built a lecture hall, pavilion, and theater. Provocative speakers were brought in, plays were staged, and blue-ribbon orchestras performed. And yet, Kinney's venture failed, culminating in an abbreviated run of *Camille* that starred the world's then-best-known stage actress, Sarah Bernhardt. It turned out that visitors to Venice preferred the sand and sidewalks to the insides of a theater. To salvage his investment, Kinney filled in most of the canals and built a miniature beach-hugging railroad and an amusement park. And, rather than the high cultural Mecca he envisaged, Venice became known as the "Coney Island of the West." It fell into decrepitude by the 1950s, when it was dubbed "a slum by the sea." The cheap rents, coupled with this quirky history, made it the logical place for Beatnik culture to flourish in Los Angeles. It was, and still is, the place most attractive to runaways, juvenile delinquents, gangs, the homeless, and the mentally ill in Southern California.

Beatnik chronicler Lawrence Lipton, who lived in Venice West, singled out the Wind Blue Inn as the crossroads of the Los Angeles underworld and the bohemians. The grungy oceanfront bar was run, said Lipton, "by a strapping bull-dyke" named "Big Fanny." All self-respecting Beatniks hung out here or any of the many coffeehouses in the area.[7] According to *The Beat Generation Map of America*, the Beatniks of Los Angeles hung out at the Grant Hotel (on Windward Court in Venice), St. Mark's Hotel (Pacific Avenue), Venice West Espresso (Oceanfront Walk, in Venice), The Wind Blue Inn (Ocean-front Walk, in Venice), Cosmo Alley (Venice), Bird in the Basket (27th & Central, a Los Angeles jazz club), Finale Jazz Club ("Little Tokyo"), and the Lighthouse (a Hermosa Beach jazz club where the West Coast cool jazz originated).[8] According to Roger McGuinn, then a young folk musician, the Beatniks who were still around in the early 1960s also gravitated to the Sunset Strip folk-music clubs, notably the Unicorn and Ciro's, where the earliest version of the Byrds took flight. As the Beatnik aura trickled down to Hollywood, Lawrence Lipton noted, "The sale of bongo drums was booming on Hollywood Boulevard. Staying up all night with jazz on the hi-fi, pounding the bongo drums and running around with beat characters was beginning to show up in the courts as grounds for divorce in filmland."[9]

Provincetown, Massachusetts

Provincetown is an isolated art colony at the tip of Cape Cod that had been a favorite among New York theater people dating back to the early twentieth century, with the establishment of the influential Provincetown Players by a group led by George Cram Cook in 1915. A veritable Who's Who of America's bohemians were attracted to Cape Cod by this theater company, including Edna St. Vincent Millay, Djuna Barnes, Louise Bryant, painter Marsden Hartley, as well as many contributors to the leftist journal *The Masses*: editor Max Eastman, the Greenwich Village bohemian and later chronicler of the Russian Revolution, John Reed, Floyd Dell, and Harry Kemp (aka "the Hobo Poet"). Most notably, Eugene O'Neill showed up in Provincetown in 1916 with a trunk full of plays. The Provincetown Players became an established troupe by putting on O'Neill's earliest plays, further bringing notoriety to this oasis of free thinking. Around this initial core of creativity, other artistic and maverick types began to gravitate to the Cape from New York, Boston, and elsewhere. Among these was a large core of homosexuals, who basked in the openness here (as they would later on Fire Island, off the southern coast of Long Island), as well as nudists, who found the isolation of the mountainous sand dunes and the calm swimming waters to their liking. Liza Lehrman, a painter affiliated with the Art Students League in New York, visited Provincetown during the summer of 1950, where she met and began an affair with Beat intimate Lucien Carr. Of this visit, she wrote,

> We were overwhelmed by the gay life that seemed to be a part of everything. When we went to a cabaret, we heard a man sing "lover back up to me" and "a hard man is good to find.". . . That was the first overt homosexual entertainment I had ever seen. In the 1940s gay men were called fags, fairies, nelly boys, pansies and so on. Not much encouragement for being out.[10]

Black Mountain, North Carolina

Black Mountain College was founded near Asheville in 1933 as an experimental school, emphasizing manual labor, and handicrafts as well as the arts (literature, music, dance, studio). The faculty included some members peripherally associated with the Beats, including poets Charles Olson and Robert Creeley, and artists Franz Kline, Robert Motherwell, Philip Guston, Kenneth Noland, and Robert Rauschenberg, whose abstract expressionist designs adorned covers and pages of Beat publications. The school was not accredited and chronically low on funds, but the students and faculty found the isolated setting and unconventional lifestyle and ideas so appealing that it managed to stay open until 1957. Once it disbanded, many of the 1,200 students and faculty went on to shape the avant-garde in America during the next decades, especially dancer-choreographer Merce

Cunningham, composer John Cage, and visionary Buckminster Fuller. In 1955–1957 Creeley edited the *Black Mountain Review*, and during that time he served as a link to Beat writers, getting work by Kerouac, Ginsberg, Burroughs, and Gary Snyder published in the influential journal. Among Black Mountain students who were included in Beat anthologies were Denise Levertov, Fielding Dawson, Edward Dorn, Jonathan Williams, and Robert Duncan. Black Mountaineers were not Beatniks per se, but they were kindred spirits. Generally more intellectual and academic than the Beats, they were described by Gregory Corso as "hip squares."[11] Dawson wrote an account of his four years at the school, in *The Black Mountain Book*, in which he described the hard labor students were required to do to pay their tuition, as well as the inspirational lectures by Olson. The 6-foot 7-inch Olson was nicknamed "Cyclops" by the students.

Chicago

Long before Beatniks set up shop on the Near North Side, the Windy City nurtured a bohemian scene. Such quintessential American figures as poet-troubadour-vagabond Vachel Lindsay and renegade poet Maxwell Bodenheim gravitated here in the early twentieth century. Eventually, both moved on (Bodenheim becoming a leading figure in New York's bohemian scenes), but not before planting creative seeds. Bodenheim teamed with Ben Hecht to produce the *Chicago Literary Times* in 1923. Along with Carl Sandburg and Harriet Monroe, Hecht and Bodenheim sparked the sort of unusual events that would become a staple of the Beatniks. At one event, Hecht and Bodenheim held a debate called "Resolved: That People Who Attend Literary Debates Are Imbeciles." Hecht opened with "The affirmative rests." Bodenheim's rebuttal was "You win." That was the end of the debate.[12] Hecht wrote about this, and other moments of pre-Beatnik counterculture, in books like *1001 Afternoons in Chicago* and *Jazz and Other Stories of Chicago Life*. Around the same time in Chicago, Margaret Anderson and her assistant "jane heap" started *The Little Review*, which was modeled on *The Masses* in New York and had the motto "Making No Compromise with the Public Taste." The magazine, which started in 1914 and folded in 1929, attracted a circle of bohemian writers and launched the careers of Hart Crane, Sherwood

Anderson, and Djuna Barnes. *The Little Review* published James Joyce's *Ulysses* for the first time—before Sylvia Beach, who generally gets credit—running it in installments for three years. Margaret Anderson shocked "straight" society with her pronouncement, "I am no man's wife, no man's delightful mistress, and I will never, never, never be a mother."[13] Waves of black Americans from the South also came to Chicago looking for work during the Great Depression and turned it into a vibrant musical center for jazz and blues. In this same migration came a number of black writers, many of whom joined the government-sponsored Illinois Writers Project, based in Chicago. Among these were Richard Wright, Margaret Walker, Willard Motley, Frank Yerby, and Arna Bontemps, spawning a black renaissance in the Midwest. Also on the writers project were Nelson Algren, Jack Conroy, Saul Bellow, Sam Ross, and Louis "Studs" Terkel. Algren, in particular, was an influence on the Beat Generation writers, with his graphic accounts of urban turbulence in novels like *Somebody in Boots* (1935), *A Walk on the Wild Side* (1956), and *The Man with the Golden Arm* (1949). The accurate depiction of morphine addiction in the latter was an influence on the work of William S. Burroughs. There was a seedy, criminal tinge to Chicago that also appealed to Burroughs when he lived here in 1942, as well as Lucien Carr, David Kammerer, and Herbert Huncke, who all lived there simultaneously before moving to New York.

According to veteran folk musician Art Thieme, "The No Exit was an old beatnik coffeehouse (served unique coffee concoctions in the 50s before anybody else in Chicago). It had chess boards inlaid into the top of every table. It was in to be awake rather than sedated (as with alcohol). 'Unique' paintings were on the walls. Beatniks were, if nothing else, literary."[14] Other Beatnik venues cited by Thieme were the Earl of Old Town, the Quiet Night, the Gate of Horn (where Lenny Bruce performed), Barbarossa, Somebody Else's Troubles, the Yellow Unicorn, the College of Complexes, and Monmartre. Add to that the presence of deejay Ken Nordine who by the late 1950s was "improvising bits of poetic prose and clever narrative pieces with jazz music, not in the hipster idiom but in something of the same spirit. He called it Word Jazz."[15] The emergence of *Playboy* magazine, published in Chicago, also fell under the Beatnik umbrella, according to Lipton who described it as "a café society scene gone beat in *Playboy* fashion."

German American artist Karl-Heinz Meschbach was drawn to Chicago in the early 1960s. Though he would later become renowned for his association with the "hippie" underground newspaper the Chicago *Seed*, Meschbach felt more connection to the Beatniks. He recalled,

> When I first came to the U.S., some years before the birth of the Hippie, I worked in Uptown Chicago which then was considered Bohemian. It held a wonderful attraction and fascination for me. Brilliance instead of vague or "Engstirnige" (close-minded) slogans. . . . Being an artist is what I wanted to do since the age of 8. I escaped East Germany, making it out on the second attempt and emigrated to the U.S. in 1962. I had aunts, uncles in Chicago, which was a very multicultural place then. I was in the U.S. Army from 1963 to 1966. . . . That's part of immigrating and being young, making yourself available to the country that takes you in. . . . I got out of the military, married and quickly got divorced. I was a lonely little bugger at that point, so I went down to Old Town looking for friends, they pointed me in the direction of the *Seed*. I showed them some of my pen and ink drawings. They seemed to like them, so I was a happy camper. Uptown, is the Near North, around Wells and Lincoln Avenues. Most of the activity would logically have been around the University of Chicago.[16]

Seattle

The Pacific Northwest had a strong tradition of labor union activism, which helped spawn a countercultural mentality that was a bit more political than the San Francisco or Los Angeles scenes. The epicenters for this activity was Pioneer Square, aka "Skid Road," and the University District, along University Way NE (nicknamed "The Ave"), where the sprawling campus of the University of Washington was found. The primary venues for Beatniks and folk-music aficionados (often an overlap in these groups) were the Pamir House, or the "P" House (at 41st Street and University Way NE), and the Eigerwand, a coffeehouse between 42nd and 43rd. The Place Next Door, the Door, and the Matador were also popular with young and restless bohemians.

New Orleans

In New Orleans Lawrence Lipton singled out Robert Cass for starting the magazine, *Climax: A creative review in the jazz spirit* in 1955.
At the same time, Cass opened a club and art gallery called the
Climax Jazz, Art & Pleasure Society of Lower Basin Street. Cass's
journal and club served as the magnet for bohemian and Beatnik
activity in New Orleans. It was also one of the few openly integrated
clubs in the South.

Beats Abroad

While the Beat Generation began as an American phenomenon, it
was adopted and adapted by artists and writers elsewhere. The American circle of Beats was unusually well traveled. Allen Ginsberg, for
example, lived for periods of time in India, Mexico, Paris, and all over

*The Beat Generation and the Beatnik phenomenon spawned a wave of publi-
cations for the general reader. Among the best were* The Beats *(1960), an anthology selected, edited, and annotated by Seymour Krim, and* The Holy
Barbarians *(1959) by Lawrence Lipton. Both provided insider looks of the bohemian scenes on the East and West Coasts, respectively.* The Beat Generation
and The Angry Young Men *(1958) tried to expand the Beat Generation to
include British writers. (Courtesy of Tom Hearn.)*

the United States, much of the time joined by Peter Orlovsky. William Burroughs lived in Tangier, Paris, Mexico City, and Texas and traveled extensively throughout South America. Gregory Corso lived in Paris, in the same "Beat Hotel" (on Rue Git-le-Coeur) as Burroughs, Ginsberg, and Orlovsky. Jack Kerouac traveled to all of these places to visit his friends and lived on Long Island, Cape Cod, and in Florida. Gary Snyder lived in Japan for years while he studied Zen Buddhism.

However, writers of other nationalities stood under the Beat umbrella, though often their only similarities to the American Beats were that they were unconventional, young, rebellious, and determined to thwart literary, social, and cultural traditions. Almost all of both nationalities' writers were men, belying a chauvinistic tendency that would be blown aside by the cultural revolutions of the 1960s. Among these were a group of British writers known as the Angry Young Men, who were forever associated with the Beats thanks to a popular anthology that was published in 1958, *The Beat Generation and the Angry Young Men*, edited by Gene Feldman and Max Gartenberg. Their unifying feature, according to the editors, was that they were all "hipsters." In the front of the book, the hipster is defined as

> a man without a country, who digs everything is shocked by nothing, whose greatest demand upon society is that it permit him to indulge in his own "kicks" unmolested. Riotously funny at times, deadly serious at others, often brutal but always pointed, these Beat and Angry young men are the logical spokesmen for our confused and confusing Atomic age.

Further, both literary circles were called a "social phenomenon" that "may well be the advance columns of a vast moral revolution, one which will transform man from a creature of history to a creature of experience."[17] The Angry Young Men, however, were more interested in political, class, and labor issues, more inclined toward socialism than Zen Buddhism, more inclined toward alienation than ecstasy, toward mockery and satire than metaphysics.

The most famous, and angriest, of the Angry Young Men was John Osborne, a playwright who touched the third rail of class in such plays as *Look Back in Anger* (1956) and *The Entertainer* (1957). Other members of this group were novelists Kingsley Amis (*Lucky Jim*), John Braine (*Room at the Top*) and J. P. Donleavy (*The Ginger Man*), who was actually an expatriate American living in Ireland. Colin Wilson further delineated this group with his influential book-length meditation, *The Outsider* (1956).

Some British writers and artists established direct connection to the Beats, through William Burroughs, who collaborated with both Brion Gysin and Ian Sommerville when they lived together at the Beat Hotel in Paris.

In 1945 William S. Burroughs and Jack Kerouac (using the pseudonyms Will Dennison and Mike Ryko, respectively) collaborated on a hard-boiled detective novel called *And the Hippos Were Boiled in Their Tanks*, based in part on Lucien Carr's stabbing of David Kammerer. The novel was finally published in 2009.

In Scotland a small circle of writers came to be associated with the Beats. Chief among these was Alexander Trocchi, whose *Cain's Book* detailed his own precipitous fall into heroin addiction.

Notes

1. Fred McDarrah and Timothy McDarrah, *Kerouac and Friends: A Beat Generation Album* (New York: Thunder's Mouth, 2002), 48.
2. Allen Ginsberg, journal entry [favorite beat bars], in *Journals Mid-Fifties, 1954–1958*, ed. Gordon Ball (New York: HarperCollins, 1995).
3. Lawrence Ferlinghetti and Nancy J. Peters, *Literary San Francisco* (San Francisco: City Lights Books/Harper and Row, 1980), 166.
4. Mudcat Café, www.mudcat.org.
5. *Beat Generation Map of America* (N.p.: Aaron Blake, 1987).
6. Steven Watson, *The Birth of the Beat Generation: Visionaries, Rebels, and Hipsters, 1944–1960* (New York: Pantheon, 1995), 189–194.
7. Lawrence Lipton, *Holy Barbarians* (New York: Julian Messner, 1959), 124.
8. *Beat Generation Map of America*.
9. Lipton, *Holy Barbarians*, 126–127.
10. Liza Williams, "Another Pretty Face," in *The Rolling Stone Book of the Beats: The Beat Generation and American Culture*, ed. Holly George-Warren (New York: Hyperion, 1999), 303.

11. Lipton, *Holy Barbarians*, 131.
12. Library of Congress, *Literary Companions* (San Francisco: Pomegranate, 1996).
13. Arthur Knight and Kit Knight, eds., *Beat Angels* (California, PA: Self-published, 1982), 9.
14. Art Thieme, "Art's Place," http://rudegnu.com/art_thieme.html.
15. Lipton, *Holy Barbarians*, 125.
16. Karl-Heinz Meschbach, interview with author, February 2008.
17. Gene Feldman and Max Gartenberg, eds., *The Beat Generation and the Angry Young Men* (New York: Dell, 1959), 12.

Conclusion

It is hard to imagine how the events of the 1960s could have unfolded as they did without the Beat Generation and the Beatniks loosening the bonds of the mainstream culture and opening the doors of perception to new alternatives. By comparison to the 1960s, the 1950s were a vast frozen expanse, buffeted by the winds of the Cold War and McCarthyism, bothered by the fears of communism and nuclear annihilation, and bewildered by political paranoia and cultural conformity. Under such conditions, the chances of pulling off a countercultural revolution were slim. And yet, that revolution did occur, though the enormity of it has only now begun to be appreciated in the wake of the much more colorful and dramatic events of the 1960s.

In every aspect of that tumultuous decade of the 1960s—in music, art, dance, literature, as well as in spirituality, environmentalism, civil rights, feminism, gay liberation, fashion, language—the fingerprint of the Beats and the Beatniks can be found. Indeed, Jack Kerouac's *On the Road* may have introduced young Americans to the possibilities of their own country, but his novel *The Dharma Bums* sparked a "rucksack revolution," blazing the trail for the back-to-nature and communal movements that were inspired by the *Whole Earth Catalog*, first published by Stewart Brand in 1968. Brand has admitted that he was influenced by the writings of Jack Kerouac and Gary Snyder, and their influence runs through the catalog's pages. The influence of the *Whole Earth Catalog*, in turn, was said to inspire computer visionaries like Steve Jobs, founder of Apple, Inc., who claimed the catalog was the "conceptual forerunner of the World Wide Web." While it's a stretch to say that, like Al Gore, Jack Kerouac and Gary Snyder "invented the Internet," their influence was there from the start, like ripples in a pond that led to the tidal wave of instant communication that washes over us today.

If the 1960s counterculture could be said to have ambassadors—people who spread the word, planted the seeds wherever they went—it would have to be the Grateful Dead. This tirelessly itinerant band famously spawned an equally itinerant group of followers, who became known as Deadheads. Together, the band and their followers would traverse the country, descending on each city in the tour itinerary and setting up camp there for a day or two. Jerry Garcia, lead guitarist and spiritual figurehead of the Grateful Dead, was quite forthright on the influence that the Beats had on him. Parke Puterbaugh noted, "According to Garcia, the transient life of touring that gave rise to the Deadhead phenomenon was largely inspired by [Jack Kerouac's novel] *On the Road*." Garcia told him, "I read it and fell in love with it, the adventure, the romance of it, everything.... I owe a lot of who I am and what I've been and what I've done to the beatniks from the Fifties and to the poetry and art and music that I've come in contact with." Garcia once said that had he not met Neal Cassady in 1963–1964, the Grateful Dead may never have existed. "Until I met Neal," Garcia told an interviewer, "I was heading toward being a graphic artist ... He helped us be the kind of band we are, a concert not a studio band."[1]

Bob Weir, the rhythm guitarist of the Grateful Dead, grew close to Neal Cassady, the model for Kerouac's Dean Moriarty in *On the Road*. Cassady accompanied the Dead on some of their early tours, and he became part of the act as well. Weir recalled, "Sometimes he would just take the stage, and he and his girlfriend had a sort of standup routine where they'd rave at each other.... Cassady kept developing, Kerouac ... only caught the budding Neal Cassady but never caught him in full bloom."[2]

Similarly, the original spelling of the Beatles was "Beetles," as a tribute to Buddy Holly's band, the Crickets. Among the many explanations for the change was that John Lennon became enamored of the Beat Generation writers and like the multidimensional aspects of "Beat" (including its echo of rock's 4/4 rhythm) rather than "Beet." George Harrison was infatuated with the recordings of Beatnik comedian Lord Buckley (see chapter 3) and could recite passages from his soliloquies. Harrison later wrote "Crackerbox Palace" (a hit single in 1977); the title was taken from the name that Lord Buckley had given to his house.

Other rock 'n' roll figures caught on to Buckley after his death, via his recordings. Among his biggest after-the-fact fans were the British blues-rock band the Yardbirds (who wrote the song "The Nazz Are Blue" in his honor) and Todd Rundgren (who named his first band the Nazz in tribute to Buckley's most famous stage routine). Beat writer William S. Burroughs had his share of rock fans, including David Bowie, who compared his stage persona Ziggy Stardust to Burroughs's novel *Nova Express*. The band Steely Dan took their name from a sexual device ("Steely Dan III from Yokohama") invented by Burroughs in his novel *Naked Lunch*. And the British progressive rock band the Soft Machine took their name from the title of a Burroughs novel.

Other Bay Area musicians, including Paul Kantner and Grace Slick of the Jefferson Airplane, and members of the Quicksilver Messenger Service, had acknowledged that the Haight-Ashbury hippie scene "was basically an outgrowth of the Beat Generation in North Beach."[3]

The influence of the Beats and beatniks was not just felt in the Bay Area. It was an international phenomenon. Roy Harper, arguably the most revered British folksinger and songwriter of the past forty years, has talked at length about this disconnect among the artists of the 1960s from their true roots in the Beat movement of the 1950s. Harper and Bob Dylan were born within days of each other, and Harper has often been compared to Dylan; he has that kind of stature in the United Kingdom.

In 2001 Harper was interviewed by the author, and this exchange took place:

Q: I don't want to flog this Bob Dylan thing too hard, but many years ago you were characterized as "the British Bob Dylan." Did you ever see yourself as operating under the same time frame, competing with Dylan for air space, so to speak?

Harper: Well, I was more attracted to poetry during the time that he was making his name in folk music. I think there's a crucial difference between us in that I've maintained what I first set out to do. Bob Dylan was fundamentally attached to the folk scene at the beginning of his life in music. He was attached to people like, say, Woody Guthrie.

Q: Yes, he made that connection very much a part of his public identity.

Harper: Whereas I was much more attached to Jack Kerouac and the Beat poets. So although I'm sort of a Brit—and I say that guardedly because I am also of the world these days—I seriously thought the answer to modern social problems was to be found in how Jack Kerouac dealt with the world in those days. Not that he dealt with it with any particular success, ultimately … in fact, he was dead by the age of 47 … drink mainly. But he and the other Beats gave me such an inspiration at the time inside which to work. From an early age, I was attached to the English romantic poets.

Q: Shelley and Keats and Byron?

Harper: Not Byron, but Shelley and Keats most definitely. Wordsworth was okay, too. And so I was attached to that poetic vision from boyhood. But then the Beat poets hit me like the proverbial sledgehammer, and that was the direction I went off in. I spent from the age of 13 or 14 to the age of 21, those crucial seven years, writing poems and being my own version of a Beat poet. In fact, you could have called me in those days a Beatnik.[4]

Just as a long list of cultural figures wielded influence on the members of the Beat Generation, the creative "Beatnik" spark was passed along to another long list of cultural figures. The following is a list of other creative individuals who, besides Harper, have cited the Beats as an influence on their work and on the ways they perceived the world:

Kathy Acker: American experimental novelist influenced by William Burroughs, best known for *Blood and Guts in High School* (1984).

Eric Andersen: Greenwich Village folksinger inspired by the Beats; addressed the connection in the two-CD set *Beat Avenue* (2003).

Laurie Anderson: Avant-garde composer and artist who has worked with William S. Burroughs.

Lester Bangs: Rock critic, singer, force of nature.

John Perry Barlow: Internet pioneer and Grateful Dead lyricist.

Richard Brautigan: San Francisco Bay Area novelist best known for *Trout Fishing in America* (1967).

Anatole Broyard: Mixed-race critic and columnist, whose memoir *When Kafka Was the Rage* covered the Beat scene he witnessed but only peripherally took part in.

Charles Bukowski: Los Angeles underground poet, novelist, and horse-track habitué.

John Cale: Rock musician (Velvet Underground) who set Kerouac's writing to music.

Jim Carroll: New York poet, singer, and writer best known for *The Basketball Diaries.*

Exene Cervanka: Singer for the Los Angeles punk band X.

Francis Ford Coppola: Film director who bought the movie rights to *On the Road*.

Robert Crumb: American underground comix artist.

Johnny Depp: Actor who purchased Jack Kerouac's raincoat.

Matt Dillon: Actor who has recorded some narration of Beat literature.

John Doe: Member of Los Angeles punk band X and underground film actor.

Robert Downey Sr.: Underground filmmaker (*Putney Swope, Chafed Elbows*).

Bob Dylan: Greenwich Village folksinger who became the best and most prolific songwriter of his generation; Dylan said, "It was Ginsberg and Jack Kerouac who inspired me at first." The long lines and visionary incantations of his song "A Hard Rain's a-Gonna Fall" were inspired by Ginsberg's "Howl."

Ramblin' Jack Elliott: Greenwich Village folksinger who befriended Jack Kerouac.

Marianne Faithfull: British singer who performed on Beat tribute recordings.

Peter Fonda: Film actor.

Jerry Garcia: Rock musician (Grateful Dead) who befriended Neal Cassady.

Jack Gelber: American playwright whose *The Connection* (1959), about heroin addiction, was a controversial hit at the Living Theatre in New York.

John Giorno: American poet who has worked with William Burroughs.

Philip Glass: Preeminent contemporary American composer, worked with David Amram and Allen Ginsberg (on *Hydrogen Jukebox*).

Paul Goodman: New York intellectual who gained fame with *Growing Up Absurd: Problems of Youth in the Organized System* (1960).

Kim Gordon: Rock musician (Sonic Youth).

Bill Griffith: Underground comix creator best known for *Zippy the Pinhead*.

George Harrison: Rock musician (Beatles) enamored of Lord Buckley.

Richard Hell: Punk musician, poet, and novelist (*Go Now*).

Nat Hentoff: *Down Beat* magazine and *Village Voice* jazz critic and civil libertarian.

Abbie Hoffman: Political radical and author (*Steal This Book*).

Dennis Hopper: Film actor and director (*Easy Rider, The Last Movie*).

Robert Hunter: Lyricist for the Grateful Dead.

Chryssie Hynde: Rock singer/songwriter (the Pretenders).

Jim Jarmusch: Underground filmmaker (*Stranger in Paradise, Down by Law*).

Lenny Kaye: Rock critic, archivist (*Nuggets*), and musician (Patti Smith Group).

Ken Kesey: American novelist best known for *One Flew Over the Cuckoo's Nest* (1962) and his association with Beat legend Neal Cassady in the 1960s.

Alfred Leslie: Painter, filmmaker who directed *Pull My Daisy*, the Beat film classic.

Ron Loewinsohn: Bay Area poet.

Lewis MacAdams: Los Angeles poet, journalist, and activist who has written extensively about the Beats.

Ray Manzarek: Musician (the Doors); collaborator with Beat poet Michael McClure.

Rod McKuen: American poet.

Jonas Mekas: Film critic and underground filmmaker in New York.

David Meltzer: Poet who took part in the San Francisco Renaissance.

Richard Meltzer: Rock critic, poet, singer.

Natalie Merchant: Singer for the rock band 10,000 Maniacs.

Barry Miles: Biographer (Ginsberg, Burroughs) and hippie scenemaker.

Jim Morrison: American poet, rock singer (the Doors), and filmmaker whose vision was inspired by Rimbaud, Aldous Huxley, and the Beats.

Joel Oppenheimer: Black Mountain poet and, later, *Village Voice* columnist.

Graham Parker: British rock singer, peerless narrator of Beat literature recordings.

Harvey Pekar: Underground comix creator best known for *American Splendor*.

Charles Plymell: San Francisco poet; friend of Allen Ginsberg and Neal Cassady.

Iggy Pop (James Osterberg): Rock singer (the Stooges).

Richard Pryor: Comedian, influenced by Lenny Bruce.

Lee Ranaldo: Member of rock band Sonic Youth.

John Rechy: American novelist best known for *City of Night* (1963).

Ishmael Reed: American poet and novelist.

Lou Reed: New York rock musician (Velvet Underground) and poet.

Henry Rollins: Rock singer (Black Flag, Rollins Band) and writer.

Hugh Romney: Greenwich Village poet who later assumed his "Wavy Gravy" persona.

Aram Saroyan: Author of book on Beat legend Lew Welch; son of William Saroyan.

Hubert Selby Jr.: Novelist best known for *Last Exit to Brooklyn* (1960) whose work has appeared in Beat anthologies.

Shel Silverstein: Children's book author, poet, songwriter, Greenwich Village fixture.

Patti Smith: Poet, rock musician, and singer; collaborator with William Burroughs.

Susan Sontag: American intellectual and novelist; definer of "camp."

Gilbert Sorrentino: New York poet, novelist, and intellectual whose work has appeared in Beat anthologies.

Terry Southern: American screenwriter and novelist who defied the censors (*Candy, The Magic Christian, Dr. Strangelove, Easy Rider*).

Michael Stipe: Singer for the rock band REM.

Joe Strummer: Front man for the rock band the Clash.

Hunter S. Thompson: American writer whose "gonzo journalism" was inspired by the writing of Jack Kerouac.

Nick Tosches: Rock critic, biographer (Sonny Liston, Jerry Lee Lewis).

Gus Van Sant: Underground filmmaker (*Drugstore Cowboy*, which featured William Burroughs).

Tom Verlaine: Member of the art-rock band Television.

Tom Waits: American singer/songwriter and actor.

Mike Watt: Rock musician and composer (the Minutemen).

John Wieners: American poet.

The process worked in reverse, now and again, as well. Take the case of the federal judge Julius S. Hoffman. Judge Hoffman became a perhaps unwitting champion of Beat literature when he ruled that the contents of Chicago's *Big Table* magazine were not obscene and, thus, copies of it could be shipped through the U.S. mail. The publication, which was started by the former staff of the *Chicago Review* after that journal was suppressed, had been held up by an obscenity lawsuit. In his opinion rejecting the suit, Judge Hoffman called Kerouac's writing "a wild prose picnic" and said Burroughs's *Naked Lunch* excerpts "intended to shock contemporary society, in order perhaps to better point out its weaknesses and flaws." And yet 10 years later, this same Judge Hoffman would be cast as a villain to the 1960s counterculture, when he presided over the Chicago Seven conspiracy trial of Abbie Hoffman, Jerry Rubin, Tom Hayden, and others. One of the witnesses for the defense at that trial was, in fact, the Beat icon Allen Ginsberg, who had become an elder statesman for the next generation.

> In 2004 the original "scroll" manuscript of Jack Kerouac's *On the Road* was auctioned at Christie's. Jim Irsay, owner of the NFL's Indianapolis Colts, made the winning bid at $2,200,000, which exceeded the preauction estimate by more than a million dollars.

Notes

1. Parke Puterbaugh, "The Beats and the Birth of the Counterculture," in *The Rolling Stone Book of the Beats: The Beat Generation and American Culture*, ed. Holly George-Warren (New York: Hyperion, 1999), 357–363.
2. Ibid.
3. Ibid.
4. Interview with the author, June 2001.

Biographical Sketches

Beat Men

Ray Bremser

Convicted for armed robbery in New Jersey in 1952, Ray Bremser (1934–1998) began writing poetry in prison, some of which LeRoi Jones published in *Yugen*. In 1960 Bremser told Donald Allen, editor of *The New American Poetry*, that "The best poets alive are me, Ginsberg, Jones, Kerouac, Orlovsky & Corso."[1] His wife, Bonnie Frazer, was also a published poet; she wrote the chronicle of her Beat years, *Troia: Mexican Memoirs*.

Note

1. Donald Allen, ed., *The New American Poetry* (New York: Grove Press, 1960), 428.

William S. Burroughs

Born into privilege in St. Louis, novelist William S. Burroughs (1914–1997) was the unwitting beneficiary of the genius of his grandfather who in 1888 patented the first key-operated adding machine, the Arithmometer. The profits from the invention trickled down to his grandson and namesake. As hard as he tried to conceal it, Burroughs was dependent on his family connections. For much of his adult life, he received a $200 monthly stipend from a trust fund, allowing him to lead the itinerant, profligate life about which he would write. At a young age, he was attracted to guns and explosives and influenced by Jack Black's *You Can't Win*, a memoir that plumbed the hobo life of the 1930s. After graduating from Harvard in 1936, Burroughs went to study psychology in Vienna. When the Nazis began to assert themselves in Austria, Burroughs moved back to the United States. By 1942 he had moved to Chicago where he worked as a store detective and bug exterminator and enrolled at the University of Chicago. There he met Lucien Carr, through David Kammerer, whom he knew from St. Louis. When Carr and Kammerer moved to New York in 1943 (Carr to enroll at Columbia, Kammerer to pursue Carr), Burroughs followed. He met Jack Kerouac and Allen Ginsberg through Carr and Kammerer and served as an older mentor to the group. He introduced Kerouac, Ginsberg, and Carr to writers to which they weren't exposed at Columbia: William Butler Yeats, André Gide, Albert Camus, Franz Kafka, James Joyce, Wilhelm Reich, and Oswald Spengler. They formed a circle that pursued what they were, as early as 1944, calling a "New Vision" dedicated to "literature of risk."[1] These intense sessions led to the sense that they were a generation apart, reinforced by their frenetic visits to the seedier bars and nightclubs of the city. Burroughs, always attracted to the criminal world, went further than any of the others, with the exception of Herbert Huncke. One of Burroughs's criminal cronies, Huncke provided the word "Beat," with which the group would mark their territory. What began as fencing stolen goods led to addiction to morphine for Burroughs. After he married Joan Adams in 1947, they moved to Texas and then Mexico, pursuing a profligate life of drugs and dissipation. On September 6, 1951, he accidentally shot and

> After killing his wife, Burroughs pled guilty to a charge of "imprudencia criminal" and was released on bail. In 1985 he wrote that his wife's death "maneuvered me into a lifelong struggle, in which I have had no choice except to write my way out."

William S. Burroughs's original title for *Naked Lunch* was *Word Hoard*. Kerouac suggested the new title when he helped Burroughs type the original manuscript, the image taken from Kerouac's assessment that it represented "a frozen moment when everyone sees what is on the end of every fork."

killed Joan. After being released from a Mexico City jail, he wandered to South America and then Tangiers, in North Africa.

His first book, *Junky*, was published under the pseudonym William Lee and was subtitled, "Confessions of an Unredeemed Drug Addict." His next book, published as *The Naked Lunch* in France in 1959, was not published in the United States until 1965 (as *Naked Lunch*), due to a legal challenge on obscenity grounds. Once the case was won, *Naked Lunch* went on to become a cult classic.

Despite his aristocratic lineage and manners, Burroughs's work reflected his often-sordid life as an addict and a homosexual. His accomplishments would always be clouded by the deaths of his wife Joan and son and only child, William S. Burroughs III, who died of drug addiction and alcoholism. As a writer Burroughs was best known for his graphic, sometimes surrealistic depiction of heroin addiction (*Junky, Naked Lunch*), gay prostitution (*The Wild Boys, Queer*), criminality (*The Soft Machine, Nova Express*), and other outlaw activities. His writing was colored by his dystopian visions of a future world police state. Burroughs lived in Tangiers, Paris, New York and, finally, Lawrence, Kansas, where he died at 83 of natural causes, a fate that would have seemed improbable if not impossible 50 years earlier.

Note

1. Barry Miles, *Burroughs: El Hombre Invisible* (New York: Hyperion, 1993), 37–40.

Lucien Carr

Judged on literary output, Lucien Carr (1925–2005) was a minor figure (though his son Caleb went on to literary fame). However, he was the conduit through whom the three major Beat writers, Allen

Ginsberg, William Burroughs, and Jack Kerouac, met. Like Burroughs, Carr came from a wealthy St. Louis family. As a young boy, he was in a play group run by Washington University English professor David Kammerer, who became obsessed with the blond, charismatic Carr. Thirteen years his senior, Kammerer was also Carr's Boy Scout master and followed him to Phillips Andover prep school, then to Bowdoin College in Maine and to the University of Chicago, where Carr was a graduate student. There, Carr met Burroughs, who already knew Kammerer from St. Louis. Carr moved to New York in 1943, to take classes at Columbia University; again he was pursued by Kammerer. Carr met Ginsberg in Lionel Trilling's literature class at Columbia, and they became friends over literature, adopting alter egos and composing elaborate theories over beer and coffee. His and Ginsberg's intense friendship predated Ginsberg's similar attachments to Kerouac, Burroughs, and Cassady. Carr introduced Burroughs to Ginsberg. Then Kerouac met Carr in the West End bar in late 1943. Though initially jealous of Carr because women were attracted to him for his aristocratic bearing and sophistication, Kerouac quickly warmed to him; the pair, in fact, planned to join the Merchant Marine together. Carr told Ginsberg about this "romantic seaman who writes poem books."[1] Carr became infamous for his August 13, 1944, murder of Kammerer, justifying it as self-defense against a homosexual assault. He served two years of a much longer sentence and then took a job at United Press International. He continued to move within the Beat circle, but kept a lower profile.

Note

1. Steven Watson, *The Birth of the Beat Generation: Visionaries, Rebels, and Hipsters, 1944–1960* (New York: Pantheon, 1995), 36.

Neal Cassady

A Beat Generation legend, Neal Cassady (1926–1968) was a larger-than-life figure who served as Kerouac's literary muse. He was born in Salt Lake City on February 8, 1926, as his parents were passing through on their way from Denver to Los Angeles, where they planned to open a barber shop. After this business venture failed, they moved back to Denver and were divorced by the time Neal was 6. After his mother died, when Neal was 10, Cassady stayed with his father, an alcoholic who lived mostly in Denver flophouses. Though he was a gifted student with an I.Q. of 120, Cassady spent more time in pool halls than classrooms, ending up in reform school for car theft. In 1945 Cassady befriended Hal Chase, home for the summer in Denver. After his return to Columbia University in the fall, Chase—who had shared an apartment with Kerouac and Burroughs the year before—showed his New York friends letters from Cassady, whose unself-conscious flow of words impressed them. When Cassady and his wife, LuAnne Henderson, took a bus to visit Chase in New York in December 1946, the fledgling Beat circle was eager to meet this mythical figure. Cassady did not disappoint. In a few weeks time, Cassady had the whole "gang"—Kerouac, Allen Ginsberg, Hal Chase, John Clellon Holmes, William Burroughs—frantically zipping around the city, staying up all night to talk and listen to jazz.

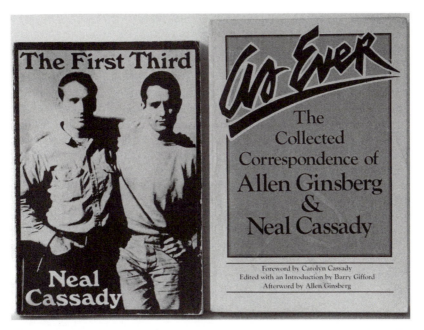

The First Third *was Neal Cassady's only attempt at serious writing. The unfinished memoirs, published posthumously by City Lights Books, features his wife Carolyn Cassady's iconic photograph of her husband (left) and Jack Kerouac at the peak of their brotherly friendship. (Courtesy of Tom Hearn.)*

Kerouac, perhaps more than any other, was captivated. His first impression of Cassady, recorded in *On the Road*, was, "a young Gene Autry—trim, thin-hipped, blue-eyed, with a real Oklahoma accent—a sideburned hero of the snowy West."[1] He saw in Cassady the impulsiveness and confidence that he lacked. As Ann Charters noted, "Cassady was a much more important influence on Kerouac than Kerouac on him."[2] In particular, Cassady's "Joan Anderson" letter to Kerouac in December 1950 helped unblock the novelist so that he was able to begin a new version of *On the Road* in April 1951. Though Cassady wrote an unfinished memoir (published posthumously as *The First Third*), some of his free-form letters can be found in the collection *As Ever: The Collected Correspondence of Allen Ginsberg and Neal Cassady* (1977). Kerouac referred to Cassady's character in *On the Road* (Dean Moriarty) as the "HOLY GOOF," writing, "I suddenly realized that Dean, by virtue of his enormous series of sins, was becoming the Idiot, the Imbecile, the Saint of the lot."[3]

Once the Beat wave passed, Cassady—after a stint in prison (1958–1960) for selling marijuana to an undercover police officer—clung to his role as "Holy Goof," finding kindred spirits with Ken Kesey's Merry Pranksters (Cassady was most famous for driving the Pranksters' psychedelic bus, "Furthur," across country). But his con man tricks, personal intensity, and prodigious drug intake burned all his bridges. In February 1968, after getting out of jail for outstanding traffic warrants, he left San Francisco and took a train to Mexico. Leaving his bag at the Celaya train station, he took a taxi to the house of a woman in San Miguel de Allende. The next day, he began walking back to Celaya to retrieve his "magic bag." On the way, he came upon a wedding party, where he washed down a number of Seconals with pulque. Thus fortified, he set out to count the railroad ties. He was found on the railroad tracks by local Indians, who claimed his last words were "64,928," apparently the subtotal of his count in progress.[4]

Notes

1. Jack Kerouac, *On the Road* (New York: Viking, 1957), 5.
2. "Enter Neal Cassady," in *The Portable Beat Reader*, ed. Ann Charters (New York: Viking, 1992), 188.
3. Kerouac, *On the Road*, 160.
4. Alan Bisbort, *Famous Last Words* (San Francisco: Pomegranate, 2001), 23.

Gregory Corso

Born in Greenwich Village to teenage parents, Gregory Corso (1930–2001) had a rough Dickensian early life. It could be argued that his life was saved by poetry. When his mother moved back to Italy, Corso was sent to an orphanage and then had five sets of foster parents all over New York City. His father eventually took him back, but Corso ran away from home, eventually sent to Bellevue for "observation." He was involved in theft and went to a reformatory; his formal education ended in sixth grade. At 16, he was convicted of robbing a finance office and sent to Clinton State Prison in Dannemora, New York, for three years. There he received the only schooling of his life. A voracious reader and autodidact, Corso plowed through works by classic poets, playwrights, and novelists like Thomas Chatterton, Christopher Marlowe, Percy Bysshe Shelley, Stendhal, Dostoevsky, and Leo Tolstoy. After his release from prison, Corso returned to Greenwich Village, where he met Ginsberg in a bar in 1950. Corso told Donald Allen: "I was graced with a deep-eyed apparition: Allen Ginsberg. Through him I first learned about contemporary poesy, and how to handle myself in an un-institutional society, as I was very much the institutional being. Beyond the great excited new joyous talks we had about poetry, he was first a gentle person and dear friend to me."[1] Because he was a misfit and a largely self-invented poet, Corso easily meshed with the other Beats. He went to Los Angeles in 1952 to work as a reporter, and shipped out as a crew member of an ocean liner. At the urging of Violet Lang, Corso moved to Cambridge, Massachusetts, to audit classes at Harvard in 1954 and 1955. Students from Harvard and Radcliffe pooled money to publish Corso's first book of poems, *The Vestal Lady on Brattle* (1955). He moved back to New York and then to San Francisco in 1956. His second book, published by Lawrence Ferlinghetti's City Lights Press, was *Gasoline* (1958), containing his popular poems "I Am 25," "The Mad Yak," and "Don't Shoot the Warthog." His controversial poem "Bomb," written while staying at "the Beat Hotel" in Paris, was first published as a broadside by City Lights in 1958, then incorporated in Corso's book *The Happy Birthday of Death* (1960). Corso incorporated older traditions of poetry—sonnet, arcane languages, mythical references—with his penchant for surrealism and the absurd. For example, his alternate titles for *The Happy Birthday of Death* included "Fried Shoes," "Flash Gordon soap," "Gargoyle liver." After the Beat wave had passed, Corso lived for periods of time in England, France, Germany, Italy, and Greece. He taught at SUNY Buffalo and the Naropa Institute in Boulder, Colorado. He wrote, "How I love to probe life. That's what poetry is to me, a wondrous prober. . . . It's not the metre or measure of a line, a breath; not 'law' music; but the assembly of great eye sounds placed into an inspired measured idea."[2] Ginsberg called him an "aphoristic poet and a poet of ideas." His verse, Ginsberg said, "is pure velvet. . . . He has been and always will be a popular

Some essential books of Beatnik verse, published between 1958 and 1961. They are by Gregory Corso (The Happy Birthday of Death), *Allen Ginsberg* (Kaddish), *Kenneth Patchen* (Because It Is), *LeRoi Jones* (Preface to a Twenty Volume Suicide Note) *and Lawrence Ferlinghetti* (A Coney Island of the Mind). *(Courtesy of Tom Hearn.)*

poet, awakener of youth, puzzlement and pleasure for sophisticated elder bibliophiles." Ginsberg also called him "Shelley's natural prophet among 'unacknowledged legislators of the world'" and Burroughs noted his "rare calling of a pure lyric gift."[3]

Notes

1. Donald Allen, ed., *The New American Poetry* (New York: Grove Press, 1960), 429–430.
2. Gregory Corso, *The Happy Birthday of Death* (New York: New Directions, 1960), dust cover.
3. Gregory Corso, *Mindfield* (New York: Thunder's Mouth, 1989), dust cover.

Robert Creeley

The Harvard-educated Robert Creeley (1926–2005) was an established poet by the time the Beat Generation got off the ground. Like Ginsberg, he was influenced by William Carlos Williams and, like Kerouac, he was a jazz aficionado. He played a pivotal role as editor of *Black Mountain Review*, which provided a vital venue for the Beats. His first book of poems was *The Gold Diggers* (1954).

Robert Duncan

An Oakland native, Robert Duncan (1919–1988) was editor of the *Experimental Review*, one of the first postwar journals to publish new American poetry. He was a major figure for more than four decades on the Bay Area literary scene and one of the first openly gay writers in America. He was one of the six poets who performed at the famed Six Gallery reading in October 1955.

William Everson (Brother Antoninus)

William Everson (1912–1994) was a conscientious objector during World War II, and was held at a work camp with other COs in Waldport, Oregon. His first book of poetry, *The Residual Years* (1948), led to a Guggenheim Fellowship. He converted to Roman Catholicism in 1948, joined the Catholic Worker Movement in 1949, and entered the Dominican Order in 1951 as a *donatus*, or lay brother without vows. Though he withdrew into the monastery, his poetry was brought to public attention by the 1957 *Evergreen Review* issue about the "San Francisco Renaissance." He became known in the press as the "Beat friar" (*Time* magazine) and was generally regarded as a Beat by association and for his generosity of spirit. His verse was inspired by Robinson Jeffers, a nature poet based in Big Sur.

Lawrence Ferlinghetti

Born in Yonkers, New York, in 1919, Lawrence Ferlinghetti served in the U.S. Navy during World War II; afterwards, he studied at the Sorbonne in Paris, where he received his doctorate. In early 1951 he moved to San Francisco to teach French, paint, and write art criticism. In 1953 he and Peter Martin opened City Lights Bookstore, its name taken from a Charlie Chaplin film. By 1955 he was the sole owner of City Lights and began a publishing company by the same name. City Lights Books published affordable paperback editions of some of the most important early works by the Beats, including Ginsberg's *Howl and Other Poems*, which initiated a major lawsuit that, when Ferlinghetti won, was a landmark in free speech. He also published Beat works by Kenneth Patchen, Kenneth Rexroth, Kerouac, Gregory Corso, Robert Duncan, Denise Levertov, and himself. His own collection of Beat-inspired poems, *A Coney Island of the Mind* (1958), published by New Directions, was one of the bestselling books of verse in American history. He, Rexroth, and Patchen began the tradition of reading their poetry to jazz accompaniment in the bars and clubs of San Francisco. In his long career, Ferlinghetti has published a dozen books of poetry, two novels, two plays, several translations, and pursued his talents as a visual artist.

Allen Ginsberg

Born Irwin Allen Ginsberg in Newark, New Jersey, in 1926, the future Beat poet extraordinaire was reared in a literary, politically active family. His father, Louis, was a poet and high school teacher, and mother Naomi, aunts, and uncles were involved with leftist political causes. Naomi suffered from chronic mental illness, and the precocious but awkward Ginsberg was neurotically sensitive to his own psychological makeup. A gifted student, he entered Columbia University on scholarship in 1943, aiming to be a labor lawyer. However, he was also a gifted poet, his talent encouraged by Columbia professors Mark Van Doren and Lionel Trilling. His visionary boundaries were further expanded by psychoanalysis, during which he examined his homosexuality and friendships with Lucien Carr, Kerouac, and Burroughs. He, Carr, and Kerouac pursued what they called "the New Vision," which Ginsberg later described as coming out "of Spengler's *Decline of the West*, which speaks of the end of the culture and the beginning of the high civilization . . . the new vision assumed the death of a square morality and replaced that meaning with belief in creativity."[1]

Like Kerouac, Ginsberg was deeply influenced by meeting Neal Cassady, who came to New York in December 1946. He fell in love with Cassady, who physically returned the favor. After Cassady returned to Denver, a smitten Ginsberg went to visit him. Kerouac followed soon thereafter. Caught in a romantic triangle with Cassady and his new girlfriend Carolyn Robinson (later Carolyn Cassady), Ginsberg returned to Columbia. By the next year, he was so immersed in his poetry that he began to have visions in which William Blake would speak to him. Fearing for his sanity, Ginsberg nonetheless welcomed the visions and incorporated them into his poetry. Seeking stability and financial independence, Ginsberg took a job at the Associated Press and continued his esoteric studies.

In January 1949 Ginsberg's generous nature prevailed when he allowed a desperate Herbert Huncke to stay at his apartment. Soon, stolen merchandise was being stored there. After being caught in a stolen car with some of Huncke's cronies, Ginsberg agreed to enter the Columbia Psychiatric Institute in July 1949, in lieu of facing criminal charges. There he met Carl Solomon, who encouraged Ginsberg's poetic "madness," against the doctors' better advice, and introduced him to the writing of "lunatics" like Jean Genet, Louis-Ferdinand Celine, and Antonin Artaud. After his release from the hospital in February 1950, Ginsberg vowed to settle down, become a lawyer, find a girlfriend, if not a wife. He took a series of jobs and found several girlfriends, but was frustrated with his writing. Enter William Carlos Williams, the modernist American poet whose dictum was "no Ideas but in things." After reading some poems Ginsberg sent him, Williams responded, "You must have a book, I shall see that you get it. Don't throw anything away. These are it."[2]

The great poet's encouragement, along with that of his friend Kerouac, refocused Ginsberg on his true life's calling. He not only turned to poetry with renewed purpose, he accepted his own homosexuality. He went to Mexico in 1953 on a prolonged trip that culminated with a move to Berkeley, ostensibly to enroll in the University of California. There, he met and fell in love with Peter Orlovsky, his lifelong companion. While working as an ad copywriter in San Francisco, Ginsberg explored his new poetic voice. The result was "Howl," which, when read publicly at the Six Gallery in San Francisco in October 1955, changed the face of modern American poetry. Rather than be destroyed by fame, as Kerouac was, or run from it, like Burroughs, Ginsberg embraced the notoriety, and controversy, that "Howl" brought to him, and used it to promote the work of his Beat companions. Over the next three decades, Ginsberg was arguably the best-known poet in the world. His other important books included *Kaddish and Other Poems* (1961), *Reality Sandwiches* (1963), *Plutonium Ode* (1982), and his collected letters and journals. Since 1969, when he began recording his arrangements of William Blake's songs, he worked with musicians as diverse as Bob Dylan, Charles Mingus, Don Cherry, the Clash, Patti Smith, and Lenny Kaye. Philip Glass composed a chamber opera, *Hydrogen Jukebox* (1993), based on Ginsberg's poems.

Notes

1. Steven Watson, *The Birth of the Beat Generation: Visionaries, Rebels, and Hipsters, 1944–1960* (New York: Pantheon, 1995), 39.
2. Ibid., 128.

Babs Gonzalez

Gonzalez (1919–1980) was a jazz musician whose "vocalese" singing style brought him to the attention of the Beats. He performed as a musician in the seminal Beat movie, *Pull My Daisy*, filmed by Robert Frank and featuring Kerouac's narration. His best-known composition was "Oop-Pop-A-Da," which became a signature song for Dizzy Gillespie. Gonzalez had some of his own poetry published in Beat literary journals.

John Clellon Holmes

Though John Clellon Holmes (1926–1988) went to Columbia University (after a stint in the Navy), he did not meet Kerouac and the other Beats until August 1948, after Kerouac had already met and hit the road with Neal Cassady. More "straight" and reserved than the rest of the Beats, Holmes served as an anchor of stability for Kerouac. Together the pair held long conversations about shared literary heroes (Dostoevsky, Balzac), listened to bebop jazz and compared notes on writing techniques and vision. They even enrolled in literature classes together at the New School on the GI Bill in 1949. Holmes eventually moved to Old Saybrook, Connecticut; his home there became a haven for Kerouac, whose great champion he became. Holmes not only helped coin the term "the Beat Generation," but he published the first bona fide "Beat" novel, *Go* (1952). In the novel, he depicted Kerouac as "Gene Pasternak," Ginsberg as "David Stofsky," and Neal Cassady as "Hart Kennedy." Many of the events he fictionally depicted were the same as those Kerouac depicted in *On the Road*, which though written soon after *Go* would not be published until five years later. Holmes further stated the case for the "Beats" in an article for the the *New York Times Magazine*, "This Is the Beat Generation," published on November 16, 1952. He wrote another novel about the Beats—specifically, their bebop jazz milieu—called *The Horn* (1958), as well as a memoir, *Nothing More to Declare* (1967) and two remembrances of his good friend, *Visitor: Jack Kerouac in Old Saybrook* (1981) and *Gone in October: Last Reflections on Jack Kerouac* (1985).

Herbert Huncke

As a 16-year-old runaway, Herbert Huncke (1915–1996) left Chicago for New York and lived by his wits as a petty thief and drug dealer in and around Times Square (he also did a three-year sentence at Sing Sing state prison). William S. Burroughs, who met Huncke in 1944 while trying to sell some morphine, began using the term "beat," which he picked up from Huncke along with a drug habit. Others in the Beat circle became fascinated with Huncke, and Kerouac credited him with inspiring the "Beat Generation" label. One of Huncke's few jobs was a brief stint as a scout for Dr. Alfred Kinsey, who was researching what would become his groundbreaking *Sexual Behavior of the Human Male* (1948). Through Huncke, Ginsberg, Kerouac, and Burroughs were all interviewed by Kinsey. Huncke inspired characters in three different Beat novels ("Elmo Hassel" in Kerouac's *On the Road*; "Herman" in Burroughs's *Junky*; and "Ancke" in John Clellon Holmes's *Go*) as well as Ginsberg's groundbreaking poem, "Howl." Holmes later told John Tytell, "We went to Huncke like you might go to Dostoevsky just because of the kind of life he had lived. He was a source, even more, a model of how to survive."[1] All told, Huncke spent 11 of his 80 years in prison. Encouraged by Ginsberg and Kerouac, he later wrote some short stories and a memoir, *Guilty of Everything* (1990), all collected in *The Herbert Huncke Reader* (1997).

> Huncke lived the last two years of his life in Room 828 of the legendary Chelsea Hotel. His rent was paid for him by the Rex Foundation, a Grateful Dead charity.

Note

1. Arthur Knight and Kit Knight, *Beat Angels* (California, PA: Self-published, 1982), 48.

Ted Joans

Poet, musician, and Beatnik impresario Ted Joans (1928–2003) was born on a Mississippi River riverboat, on which his father was an entertainer. After graduating from the University of Indiana in 1951, Joans moved to Greenwich Village to pursue a dream of becoming a bohemian painter. In November 1958 Allen Ginsberg convinced him to perform his poetry in coffeehouses, and Joans took to the role as if born to it. Part tongue-in-cheek but part business venture, Joans and photographer Fred McDarrah created a "Rent-A-Beatnik" gimmick. They would provide a real bonafide Beatnik to attend and perform at parties thrown by curious New Yorkers. Usually the rented Beatnik was Joans, who would perform his poems, like "The Sermon," which opened, "So you want to be hip little girls / You want to learn to swing." Fred McDarrah said that "His ubiquitous presence at poetry readings from New York to Paris to Timbuktu has given him guru status" as "the quintessential Beatnik."[1]

Note

1. Fred McDarrah and Timothy McDarrah, *Kerouac and Friends: A Beat Generation Album* (New York: Thunder's Mouth, 2002), 174.

LeRoi Jones

LeRoi Jones (b. 1934) was one of the few African American writers associated with the Beats. He was from Newark, New Jersey, and attended Rutgers, Howard, and Columbia universities, as well as the New School for Social Research in New York. After serving in the U.S. Air Force from 1954 to 1957, Jones moved to Greenwich Village, met and married Hettie Cohen and, with her, founded *Yugen* magazine and Totem Press. His book *Preface to a Twenty Volume Suicide Note* (1961) was an essential Beat title. Jones also edited an essential anthology called *The Moderns* (1963), of prose work by mostly Beat writers. Of the Beat vision, he wrote, "Burroughs's addicts, Kerouac's mobile young voyeurs, my own Negroes, are literally not included in the mainstream of American life. These characters are people whom [Oswald] Spengler called Fellaheen, people living on the ruins of a civilization. They are Americans no character in a John Updike novel would be happy to meet, but they are nonetheless Americans."[1] After Malcolm X was assassinated in 1965, Jones focused on "black cultural nationalism," started the Black Arts Repertory Theatre in Harlem, converted to the Muslim faith, and changed his name to Amiri Baraka. He was the poet laureate of the state of New Jersey.

Note

1. *The Portable Beat Reader*, ed. Ann Charters (New York: Viking, 1992), 339–340.

Bob Kaufman

Bob Kaufman (1925–1989) was the quintessential Beatnik poet in San Francisco, making his name for spontaneous readings at North

Beach landmarks like the Coexistence Bagel Shop. Part Jewish and part black, he was known as "the American Rimbaud," in reference to the French poet whose derangement of the senses was an influence on Beat writers. "His commitment to anarchism and freedom of expression was total," wrote Steven Watson. "And he repeatedly clashed with the police."[1] His first work, the Abomunist Manifesto (1959) was published as a broadside by City Lights Books. In 1963, he took a vow of silence that lasted ten years. When he died, his ashes were scattered in San Francisco Bay while Charlie Parker's "Just You, Just Me" played.

Note

1. Steven Watson, *The Birth of the Beat Generation: Visionaries, Rebels, and Hipsters, 1944–1960* (New York: Pantheon, 1995), 226.

Jack Kerouac

Jean-Louis Lebris de ("Jack") Kerouac (1922–1969), creator of the "Duluoz Legend" and dubbed by the media "King of the Beats," was born in Lowell, Massachusetts, on March 12, 1922. He was the youngest of three children of working-class parents. His father, Leo, was a printer and mother Gabriele (whom he called "Memere") worked on the assembly line of a shoe factory. At home, the family spoke *jual*, the patois of French Canadians, the family lineage on both sides. As late as age 11, Jack spoke "halting English" and had trouble in school. The defining event of his childhood was the death of his brother Gerard to rheumatic fever at age 9 (when Jack was 4). After Gerard died, a melancholic Jack turned to solitary pursuits, like comic books, radio shows, and fantasy baseball leagues. He also excelled in sports. A track and football star at Lowell High School, Kerouac received a scholarship to Manhattan's Horace Mann Prep School in 1939, in anticipation of playing football for Columbia University (then a college football power), which he entered in September 1940. Sensitive to being perceived as a boy from the backwoods and still awkward in speech and manners, Kerouac immersed himself in books. In his freshman year at Columbia, he broke his leg early in the football season, effectively ending his sports career.

After Kerouac lost his scholarship, he joined the Navy in February 1943. Unable to adapt to military regimentation, he received an honorable discharge after eight months and returned to New York, where he befriended Allen Ginsberg, William S. Burroughs, Lucien Carr, and Hal Chase—the initial group that would become "the Beats." He also met Edie Parker and married her in August 1944 (the marriage was annulled the following year). Feeling restless and wanting to help the war effort, he joined the Merchant Marine and took part in dangerous crossings of the North Atlantic, infested with German U-boats. After Kerouac returned to his circle of friends in New York, he worked seriously on his writing. He saw himself then as a great "sea poet" and novelist in the vein of Walt Whitman and Herman Melville.

In December 1946 Kerouac met Neal Cassady, the most important event in Kerouac's writing life. With Cassady, off and on between 1947 and 1950, Kerouac zigzagged back and forth across the country, temporarily settling in Denver, Mexico City, and San Francisco, gaining experiences that were vital to what would become his best-known writings. Between road adventures, he returned to New York to live with his mother (his father died in 1945 of stomach cancer) and write in a quiet environment. He married in 1950 to Joan Haverty, in whose apartment he wrote the first version of *On the Road* in 1951, typing it out on one long roll of paper he got from a newspaper wire machine. Kerouac's first novel, *The Town and the City*, was published in 1950. Though it was not written in the free-flowing style of *On the Road*—which Ginsberg would famously call "spontaneous bop prosody"—it was an ambitious reimagining of his boyhood in Lowell and his life in New York City. The traditional writing style and plot were modeled on the work of Thomas Wolfe, whom Kerouac revered. The book was praised by the critics though it did not sell particularly well, the first and only time this (critical praise and dismal sales) would happen to Kerouac. As a result, Kerouac was deemed a promising young American novelist.

Because he had yet to gain the notoriety of contemporaries like Norman Mailer or Gore Vidal, Kerouac could not make demands of his publisher. Thus, a heavily edited and scaled-down version of *On the Road*—which Kerouac originally titled *The Beat Generation*—was finally published in late 1957. The response was overwhelming—

bestseller lists, media exposure, marriage propositions—and Kerouac was considered hot property. Thus, he could now begin to get some of his other work published. Between the publication of *The Town and the City* and *On the Road*, Kerouac had written seven novels, two books of poetry, and hundreds of letters and journal entries, with his newfound spontaneous prose techniques. None of this—what he called the "Duluoz Legend"—was published until after *On the Road* made him a household name. His most cherished work, *Visions of Neal*, later changed to *Visions of Cody*, an expanded meditation on the frenetic life of his road companion Neal Cassady, would not be published in its entirety until four years after his death. It is with that book and the original manuscript of *On the Road* that Kerouac cemented his reputation among the literary underworld, that loose assemblage that became known as the Beat Generation. His backlog began to be published as *The Subterraneans* (1958), *Dr. Sax* (1959), *Maggie Cassidy* (1959), *Tristessa* (1960), and *Visions of Gerard* (1963).

After his overwhelming and seemingly overnight success with *On the Road*, the novel that instantly made him the "King of the Beats," Kerouac's writing suffered from his increasing reliance on alcohol. *Big Sur* (1962), his finest novel from this later period, captured his disturbed state of mind. *Vanity of Duluoz* (1968) was his last major book, published the year before he died. By then, noted critic Bruce Cook, "He had become the whipping boy of the literary establishment, reviled as much for his boyish romanticism and predilection for the seamy side of life, as for his 'overnight' success. . . . He was the protagonist of the Beat Generation, the avatar of rebellion during the Eisenhower era when rebellion was not quite the thing."[1] Ginsberg, in dedicating his most famous book, *Howl and Other Poems*, to Kerouac, called him, the "new Buddha of American prose, who spit forth intelligence into eleven books written in half the number of years . . . creating a spontaneous bop prosody and original classic literature."[2]

> Kerouac was planning his next novel when he died. It was to have been called *The Beat Spotlight*, in homage to his father's job as a printer for the Spotlight Press in Lowell, Massachusetts, where Kerouac grew up.

Notes

1. Bruce Cook, book review of Gerald Nicosia's Kerouac biography, *Memory Babe*, *Washington Post*, July 24, 1983.
2. Allen Ginsberg, *Howl and Other Poems* (San Francisco: City Lights, 1956), 3.

Tuli Kupferberg

Poet, performer, publisher, and activist, Kupferberg (b. 1923) was an established figure on the East Village scene when the Beat Generation emerged. In 1958 Kupferberg started a magazine called *Birth*, which began featuring Beat writers and artists. In 1961 he published a book called *Beatniks; or, The War Against the Beats*, which suggested that the Beats were whipping boys and scapegoats for America's own mortal fear in a post–atomic bomb age. In 1964 Kupferberg formed a satiric rock band, the Fugs, with two other East Village fixtures, Ed Sanders and Ken Weaver. The Fugs created immortal classics like "Slum Goddess," "Boobs a Lot," "CIA Man," "Kill for Peace," and "Mutant Stomp." Kupferberg entered the nation's paperback bestseller lists with his antiwar manifesto *1001 Ways to Beat the Draft*. As of 2009 the Fugs were still performing.

Philip Lamantia

One of the six poets who read at the seminal Six Gallery event in October 1955, Lamantia (1927–2005) was more of a surrealist than a Beat. He had, prior to his notoriety with his association with Ginsberg, been an editor at the important surrealist magazine *View* during the 1940s. His verse was praised by Andre Breton, author of the *Surrealist Manifesto*. He was the model for the character "Francis Da Pavia" in Jack Kerouac's bestselling novel, *The Dharma Bums*.

Michael McClure

After moving to San Francisco to study art in 1954, Michael McClure (b. 1934) was sidetracked by the Poetry Center at San Francisco State College. There, he met Ruth Witt-Diamant, the director, and Robert Duncan, a member of the so-called Berkeley renaissance. McClure participated in a performance of Duncan's play *Faust Foutu*, and met Allen Ginsberg and Gary Snyder just prior to taking part in the famous Six Gallery reading in October 1955. His first book of poems, *Passage* (1956), was published by Jonathan Williams, affiliated with Black Mountain College. McClure went on to a long, distinguished career as a poet, playwright (his play *The Beard* was a staple of the hippie era), essayist, and performer (he worked with both Jim Morrison and Ray Manzarek of the Doors). He would even ghostwrite the memoir of a Hell's Angel, *Freewheelin' Frank* (1967). He, like Ginsberg and Snyder, was an important link between the Beats and the hippies in the Bay Area. (See also interview with Michael McClure in Primary Documents.)

Jack Micheline

Author of 20 books of verse, Jack Micheline (1929–1998) was part of the vagabond tradition of pre-Beats Vachel Lindsay and Maxwell Bodenheim, calling himself "one of the last of the American troubadours." Kerouac befriended him in Greenwich Village in the 1950s and wrote an introduction to his first book of poetry, *River of Red Wine* (1958). Kerouac called Micheline "Doctor Johnson Zen Master Magee of Innisfree," and said he used the "swinging free style I like and his sweet lines revive the poetry of open hope in America." Micheline was a frequent guest at poetry readings in New York and made much needed cash as a "Rent-a-Beatnik" at suburban parties. He eventually moved to San Francisco, where he lived and died in poverty. He was born in the Bronx, named Harvey Martin Silver, but eventually changed his first name to Jack, in homage to Jack London, and added an "e" to his mother's maiden name (Michelin) to create his last name.

Ken Nordine

Ken Nordine (b. 1920) was a staple of the hipster and Beat scenes in Chicago, a prominent deejay with a distinctive voice who coined some of hip lingo under the name "word jazz." He initially attracted attention when he recorded the aural vignettes on *Word Jazz* on the Dot record label in 1957. *Word Jazz, Son of Word Jazz* (Dot, 1958), and his other albums in this vein feature Nordine's narration over jazz instrumentation. He began performing and recording such albums at the peak of the Beat movement and was associated with the poetry-and-jazz movement.

Beatnik deejay Ken Nordine's voice was so distinctive that it was featured on television commercials. He was also hired by director William Friedkin as the vocal coach for Linda Blair during the filming of *The Exorcist*.

Peter Orlovsky

Peter Orlovsky was born on the Lower East Side in 1932, the son of a Russian White Army soldier who moved the family of five children to Long Island. Both of the Orlovsky parents were alcoholics and the children suffered terrible deprivations. Two of the sons eventually were institutionalized, and Peter Orlovsky was probably rescued from a similar fate through his relationship with Allen Ginsberg. After dropping out of high school, Orlovsky joined the Army and served in the Korean War. He was assigned as a medic in San Francisco after telling an officer "an army is an army of love." There he met the painter Robert LaVigne, whose nude portrait of Orlovsky attracted Ginsberg's notice. The pair became inseparable until Ginsberg's death. Orlovsky often read his own child-like verse at readings with Ginsberg and other Beats. In 1960, when Donald Allen was compiling *The New American Poetry* anthology, Orlovsky sent a biographical note, part of which read, "Grew up with dirty feet & giggles. Can't stand dust so pick my nose. Trouble in school: always thinking dreaming sad mistry [*sic*] problems.... Love pretzels & can't remember dreams anymore. Will somebody please buy me a mountain with a cave up there." He published one book, *Clean Asshole Poems & Smiling Vegetable Poems* (No. 37, City Lights Pocket Poet Series). Joyce Johnson said, upon meeting Orlovsky, that "He seemed shockingly brand new, a person suddenly launched into a world for which he totally lacked a frame of reference."[1]

Note

1. Joyce Johnson, *Minor Characters* (Boston: Houghton Mifflin, 1983), 123.

Kenneth Rexroth

An important figure in the San Francisco Poetry Renaissance, Rexroth (1905–1982) helped build the foundation that allowed the younger Beat writers to attract a wide audience. More politically radical than the younger writers, Rexroth was a union organizer and conscientious objector during World War II. He was a columnist and critic for national magazines, often touting the West Coast literary scene. His translations of Asian verse and interest in Eastern philosophy were highly influential on Gary Snyder and Allen Ginsberg. He was a widely published poet who often read his work to jazz accompaniment. He also held weekly seminars in his apartment that brought most of the important Bay Area writers together. He was the master of ceremonies at the groundbreaking Six Gallery reading, at which Ginsberg read "Howl" for the first time and changed the face of American poetry. Rexroth was the face of Bay Area poetry when the Beats arrived. He was considered a "father figure" to the Beats, even though as Ferlinghetti noted, "he did not have reciprocal feelings." Indeed, the Beats' scruffy indifference, or lack of deference, to his stature caused Rexroth to lash out at them in print and in person. In 2008 Gary Snyder told a reporter, "Rexroth was a great mentor. He was a polymath, universalist, critical thinker, and he declared himself an anarcho-pacifist."[1]

Note

1. Dana Goodyear, "Zen Master," *New Yorker*, October 20, 2008, 68.

Ed Sanders

Poet, performer, activist, bookshop owner, and publisher, Sanders (b. 1939) hitchhiked to Greenwich Village from his native Missouri after reading *On the Road* and "Howl," determined to be a part of the nascent Beat scene. He participated in a number of antiwar and antinuclear demonstrations and organized similar events in the East Village. In 1962 he opened the Peace Eye Bookstore (on East 10th Street), which soon became a center for New York's underground and radical community. His first book, *Poem from Jail* (1963), was written on the insides of cigarette packs while incarcerated for attempting to board the Polaris-missile submarine, the *Ethan Allen*, in New London, Connecticut, as "a witness for peace." He met Tuli Kupferberg on the East Village streets, and the two formed (with Ken Weaver) a "folk rock" group called the Fugs. Sanders said the inspiration for the

Fugs ranged from "the dances of Dionysus in the ancient Greek plays" to "the jazz-poetry of the Beats, to Charlie Parker's seething sax, to the silence of John Cage, to the calm pushiness of the Happening movement, the songs of the Civil Rights movement, and to our concept that there was oodles of freedom guaranteed by the U.S. Constitution that was not being used."[1] Sanders is perhaps best-known for *The Family*, a book about Charles Manson and his followers that remains in print after more than 30 years. Sanders cemented his Beat legend with a touching appearance on William F. Buckley's *Firing Line* show in September 1968 with an inebriated Jack Kerouac. Kerouac, by then a raging anti-Communist, tried to bait the "hippie" Sanders, who gently reminded the Beat writer how much he was admired by younger writers.

Note

1. www.thefugs.com, official Web site of the Fugs.

Gary Snyder

Gary Snyder (b. 1930) was raised on a small farm north of Seattle. His grandfather was a homesteader and a "dues paying member of the Industrial Workers of the World" who voted for socialist candidates and was a big influence during Snyder's boyhood. "As early as I was allowed, at age nine or ten, I went off and slept in the woods at night alone," he later said, implying that the lure of nature was as strong as his fear of his sadistic mother, a frustrated writer. By 16 Snyder was an accomplished mountain climber, having scaled 16 major peaks, including Mount St. Helens. Jack Kerouac recounted Snyder's boyhood in *The Dharma Bums*, through his character Japhy Ryder, based on Snyder: "brought up in a log cabin deep in the woods with his father and mother and sister, from the beginning a woods boy, an axman, farmer, interested in animals and Indian lore so that when he finally got to college by hook or crook he was already well equipped for his early studies in anthropology and later in Indian myth and in actual texts of Indian mythology. Finally he learned Chinese and Japanese and became an Oriental scholar and discovered the greatest Dharma Bums of them all, the Zen lunatics of China and Japan."[1]

Snyder attended Oregon's Reed College, where he was room-
mates with poets Lew Welch and Philip Whalen, later part of the
Beat Generation circle in San Francisco. After graduating from Reed
in 1951, Snyder worked in logging camps and fire lookouts in the Pacific Northwest before enrolling in University of California at Berkeley to study Chinese and Japanese. He began serious meditation
practice in 1952 and was one of six readers at the Six Gallery event
that launched the so-called San Francisco Poetry Renaissance in
1955. At this time, he befriended Kerouac and introduced him to
mountain climbing and the joys of the wild, all of which the novelist
detailed in *The Dharma Bums*. Snyder's influence on Kerouac was positive, serving as a healthy alternative to his itinerant debauchery. His
example even inspired Kerouac to become a fire lookout the following
year.

In 1956 Snyder moved to Japan for the next several years, to
undergo training as a Zen monk and study the koan (the first koan
his master gave him was to "show what his face looked like before his
parents met."). His interest in Eastern philosophy also fascinated Kerouac, whose Japhy Ryder was one of his most appealing and enno-
bling characters. Snyder brought concerns about the environment and
Zen Buddhism into the Beat circle. He also had roots in Native
American culture and the anarchist movement. His first volume of
poetry, *Riprap*, was published in 1959. More than 15 volumes followed, and in 1975 Snyder won the Pulitzer Prize for *Turtle Island*.
His magnum opus, *Mountains and Rivers Without End* (1996), was 40
years in the making. Bruce Cook wrote, "If Allen Ginsberg was the
Beat Generation's Walt Whitman, then Gary Snyder was its Henry
David Thoreau."[2] After the Beat movement ran its course, Snyder
moved his family to an isolated cabin on San Juan Ridge, in the Yuba
River watershed, near Nevada City, California. They used solar panels
for electricity, got water from wells, burned wood for heat, communi-
cated by CB radio (no telephone), and used an outhouse. In 1966
Snyder helped organize the Human Be-In in Golden Gate Park, held
in January 1967, then addressed the first Earth Day event in Fort
Collins, Colorado, in 1970. He composed the 1969 environmentalist
manifesto, "Four Changes," in which he warned of overpopulation,
pollution, and overconsumption and distributed it for free; the document has since become a cornerstone of modern environmentalism.

He authored 19 books of poetry and prose that are, said journalist Dana Goodyear, "engaged with watersheds, geology, logging, back-packing, etho-poetics, Native American oral storytelling, communal living, sex, coyotes, bears, Tibetan deities, Chinese landscape painting, Japanese Noh drama, and the intimacies of family life." Snyder was ambivalent about his standing in the Beatnik pantheon, saying, "I'm not a Beat in a literary sense. I'm a historical part of that circle of friends, and I was part of the early sociological and cultural effect of it. My work did not fit with the critics' and the media's idea of Beat writing, ever. We were all so different from each other, all these unique cases."[3]

Notes

1. Jack Kerouac, *The Dharma Bums*, 10.
2. Bruce Cook, *The Beat Generation* (New York: Charles Scribner's Sons, 1971), 28.
3. Dana Goodyear, "Zen Master," *New Yorker*, October 20, 2008, 66–75.

Carl Solomon

Born in the Bronx, Carl Solomon (1928–1994) was influenced by French surrealists like André Breton and Antonin Artaud. In 1949 he suffered a major breakdown on his 21st birthday, checking himself into the Psychiatric Institute of New York City for shock treatments. There, he met Allen Ginsberg, who had been committed after stolen goods were found in his apartment. Solomon greeted him by saying he was "Kirillov" from *The Possessed* by Dostoevsky, while Ginsberg claimed to be "Myshkin" from Dostoevsky's *The Idiot*. Some of what Solomon told Ginsberg later found a home in his famous poem "Howl," which he dedicated to Solomon and which included the line, "and subsequently presented themselves on the granite steps of the madhouse with shaven heads and harlequin speech of suicide, demanding instantaneous lobotomy." Solomon's other Beat connection was through his uncle A. A. Wyn, publisher of Ace paperbacks. After getting out of the hospital, Solomon worked at Ace Books and convinced his uncle to publish Burroughs's first book, *Junky* (under the pseudonym William Lee). Solomon later published a book of his own writings, *Mishaps, Perhaps* (1966).

Jack Spicer

After growing up in Los Angeles, Jack Spicer (1925–1965) went to the University of California in Berkeley to study linguistics in 1945. He spent most of the rest of his writing life in the Bay Area, running a workshop at San Francisco State College called "Poetry as Magic," and being, along with Robert Duncan and Robin Blaser, part of a "Berkeley Renaissance." He also participated in, and sometimes hosted, Blabbermouth Night at a literary bar called The Place. He was hesitant to publish his poems, calling them "one night stands." As reported by his friend and fellow poet Robin Blaser, Spicer's final words on his deathbed in 1965 were "My vocabulary did this to me. Your love will let you go on." Posthumously, Spicer's literary reputation has soared as high as any writer associated with the Beat Generation.

Lew Welch

Though Lew Welch (1926–1971) was one of the lesser-known Beat poets, he was one of the most impassioned and uncompromising. The former high school track star and Army veteran was a roommate at Oregon's Reed College with Gary Snyder and Philip Whalen. He went on to do graduate work in linguistics at the University of Chicago, then worked as an ad copywriter at Montgomery Ward. He gravitated to the Bay Area after the Six Gallery reading in 1955 hailed the San Francisco Poetry Renaissance, with which his friends Whalen and Snyder were involved. He met and befriended Jack Kerouac and drove the Beat leader from San Francisco back to New York in his Jeep, along with Albert Saijo (their journal of the trip was collaboratively published as *Trip Trap* in 1959). His first solo book of poems was *Wobbly Rock* (1960). The rest of his life was obsessively devoted to following his muse. When his muse ran out, Welch disappeared among the Sierra Nevada Mountains, never to be seen again.

Philip Whalen

After serving in the U.S. Army Air Force 1943–1946, Whalen (1923–2001) went to Reed College, where he roomed with Gary Snyder and Lew Welch. As Warren Coughlin in *The Dharma Bums*, Kerouac described Whalen as "180 pounds of poet meat." A gentle spirit and genial personality, Whalen was an ordained Zen Buddhist priest and one of Kerouac's most reliable confidants and friends. His first book of poetry was *Self-portrait, from Another Direction* (1959).

Beat Women

Allen Ginsberg once likened the Beats to a "boy gang," and the metaphor was apt. Few women broke past the testosterone zone to stand on equal footing with Ginsberg, Kerouac, Burroughs, Cassady, or most of the other Beats who came along after this core group was formed. Women were treated badly by most of the men, and largely ignored by those who weren't interested in them sexually. Among the women who stood the tallest were some who, sadly, never wrote a word about their experiences.

Joan (Vollmer Adams) Burroughs

According to Steven Watson, Joan Burroughs (1924–1951) was "the sole female equal in an otherwise all-male cast."[1] When Burroughs met her, she was married and pregnant. After she had her baby (a daughter), she left her husband, a law student named Paul Adams, to get an apartment with Edie Parker (later Jack Kerouac's first wife). She turned her apartment into a literary salon of sorts, opening it unquestioningly to all the major figures of the Beat circle (Burroughs, Kerouac, Ginsberg, Huncke, Hal Chase). Extremely well read and sexually uninhibited, Vollmer pointed the way to a new lifestyle that the Beats would embrace totally. She developed a chemical dependence on Benzedrine and ended up in Bellevue Hospital. Burroughs checked her out of the hospital, and the pair took a vow of marriage (though some questions remain about whether they were ever legally married) and moved to Texas, where they had a son, William Burroughs Jr. in 1950. They moved to Mexico where, on September 6, 1951, a drunken Burroughs accidentally killed Vollmer while attempting to shoot a glass off her head with a Star .380 pistol in a botched William Tell trick.

Note

1. Steven Watson, *The Birth of the Beat Generation: Visionaries, Rebels, and Hipsters, 1944–1960* (New York: Pantheon, 1995), 57.

Carolyn Cassady

Nashville-born Carolyn Robinson (b. 1923) went to Bennington College on scholarship, studying drama, dance, and painting. After graduating from Bennington, she moved to Denver to study theater arts. There she met and was courted by Neal Cassady, who introduced her to his Beat friends Jack Kerouac and Allen Ginsberg. She moved to San Francisco to pursue a career in costume design, while Cassady hit the road with Ginsberg. In October 1947 Cassady reunited with her in San Francisco and they were married on April Fool's Day 1948. For the next several years, they lived in San Francisco, San Jose, and Los Gatos, and had three children. During this time, she provided a stable home for Cassady, as well as a haven for him after his release from prison in 1960, and a reliable way station for Kerouac during the times when he was off the road. She published two memoirs about her connections to the pair who launched the Beat Generation, *Heart Beat: My Life with Jack and Neal* (1976) and *Off the Road: My Years with Cassady, Kerouac and Ginsberg* (1990).

In the film adaptation of *Heart Beat*, Carolyn Cassady's part was played by Sissy Spacek, while Nick Nolte portrayed Neal Cassady. Jan Kerouac, Jack's daughter, was hired as an extra.

Ann Charters

Ann Charters (b. 1936) was studying for her master's degree at University of California at Berkeley when she read *The Dharma Bums* in 1958. She fell instantly under the Beat spell, attending a reenactment of the famous Six Gallery reading that year in Berkeley. She began collecting Kerouac's work in 1962. She compiled the first bibliography of his work, meeting with the novelist in 1966 to go through his files. By then, Kerouac was despairing over his neglect by the academy, which considered his writing unworthy of serious study. Charters embarked on a one-person campaign to resurrect his literary reputation. The revival began with her biography, *Kerouac* (1974), the first on the Beat legend. She stayed in contact with the Beat Generation circle, compiling literary ephemera, consulting on documentary films and editing the definitive *Portable Beat Reader* (1992). She also edited the *Portable Jack Kerouac* (1995), *Selected Letters, 1940–1956* by Jack Kerouac (1995) and *Selected Letters, 1957–1969* by Jack Kerouac (1999). For years Charters was on the English department faculty at University of Connecticut. Her *The Story and Its Writer* is one of the best-selling textbooks for college students. Of her work keeping the Beat flame alive, Charters said, "I'm not a writer. I'm an editor and a teacher. American literature has been kind to me and I want to give something back." As to why college students continue to flock to the work of Kerouac and other Beats, Charters said, "Life looks kind of bleak to them, and Kerouac is a hero because he lived on his own terms. . . . Most important, though, is that Kerouac writes so well about an America that's gone but we still have in our hearts. Jack Kerouac deserves the attention he is getting. He should have a place as a major American writer."[1]

Note

1. Alan Bisbort, "Keeper of the Beat Flame," *Hartford Advocate*, April 27, 1995, 21.

Diane di Prima

Born in 1934 and raised in Brooklyn's Italian American community, di Prima dropped out of Swarthmore College to pursue writing. She joined a group of artists in New York who called themselves the "New Bohemians" before the Beats emerged. She was a serious student of poetry, corresponding with Kenneth Patchen, Charles Olson, and Ezra Pound. In 1953 she visited Pound in St. Elizabeth's, the mental hospital in Washington, D.C., where he was sent in lieu of prison for his fascist radio broadcasts during World War II. Watson wrote, "She provided an apt combination of Beat qualities: absolute independence, wide sexual experience from mid-teens on, familiarity with drugs, the Village, jazz and bohemian style."[1] She had an affair with LeRoi Jones and had a baby daughter by him (as well as four other children). Her first book, *This Kind of Bird Flies Backwards* (1958), was published by Hettie and LeRoi Jones's Totem Press. Her second book, *Dinners and Nightmares* (1961), was a book of prose sketches dedicated to "pads and the people who shared them" and contained a blurb that boasted its "honesty would shock the romantic illusions of even the beat generation." Maurice Girodias of Olympia Press encouraged her to write *Memoirs of a Beatnik* (1969), an erotic chronicle of her intimate relations with Beat figures like Jack Kerouac and Allen Ginsberg.

> Diane di Prima, along with Gary Snyder, Allen Ginsberg and Michael McClure, forged a link between the Beats and the hippies. She lived for a spell at Timothy Leary's psychedelic commune in Millbrook, New York and settled in San Francisco, where she joined the Diggers in 1968.

Note

1. Steven Watson, *The Birth of the Beat Generation: Visionaries, Rebels, and Hipsters, 1944–1960* (New York: Pantheon, 1995), 270–272.

Joyce Johnson (née Glassman)

Joyce Glassman (b. 1935) was a Barnard College graduate and aspiring 21-year-old novelist working for publisher Robert Giroux when she met Jack Kerouac, 13 years her senior. Prior to meeting him, she had read, and been impressed by his first novel *The Town and the City*. Her Barnard classmate Elise Cowen had befriended Allen Ginsberg, who set up a blind date for Kerouac with Glassman at a Greenwich Village Howard Johnson's in January 1957. Kerouac moved into her apartment on the Upper West Side and she was his companion, and anchor, when *On the Road* was published and he was vaulted nearly overnight into international celebrity as "King of the Beats." They continued their relationship by mail whenever Kerouac would leave the city. Their correspondence was published as *Door Wide Open: A Beat Love Affair in Letters, 1957–1958* (2000). She later wrote about those days in her award-winning memoir *Minor Characters* (1983), a candid "insider" account of the Beats' inner circle. Johnson went on to write several highly acclaimed novels, including *In the Night Café* (1989).

Hettie Jones (née Cohen)

Hettie Cohen met LeRoi Jones in 1957 when he applied for a job at the *Record Changer*, where she was subscription manager. They bonded over the fact that she was reading Kafka's *Amerika*; they were married a year later. They started *Yugen* magazine in 1958 as "a new consciousness in arts and letters," and hosted gatherings of writers, artists and musicians at their Village apartment (402 West 20th Street), creating one of the few multiracial mingling spots in the city which Ginsberg described as "an acme of good feeling." She and LeRoi Jones divorced in 1965, when the latter became more involved with black activism in the wake of Malcolm X's assassination. She went on to write several children's books, direct a day-care program, and engage in antipoverty activism. Hettie Jones chronicled her days as a Beat in *How I Became Hettie Jones* (1989), an unflinching reassessment of those heady days. She has also published collections of her own verse, including *Drive*.

Lenore Kandel

Poet and Zen practitioner Lenore Kandel (b. 1932) helped, along with Gary Snyder and Allen Ginsberg, pass the Beat torch on to the so-called hippies. Carolyn Cassady called her a "fertility goddess" while Kerouac called her "a big Rumanian monster beauty, who knows everything." Though she was born and raised in New York City, Kandel was a resident of San Francisco's Haight-Ashbury at the height of "flower power." Kandel had earlier published *The Love Book* (1965), a collection of erotic verse that led to a court challenge for "obscenity." Her later book, *Word Alchemy* (1967), contained controversial poems like "First They Slaughtered the Angels."

Edith "Edie" Parker Kerouac

After growing up in wealthy Grosse Pointe, Michigan, Edith Parker (1923–1992) enrolled in Columbia University in 1941. There, she met Joan Vollmer Adams, with whom she shared an apartment that became the first literary salon of the Beats' inner circle. She dated Henry Cru, a merchant marine. When Cru shipped out, she began dating his friend, Jack Kerouac, whom she married on August 22, 1944; the marriage was annulled the following year. Parker would marry three more times and write an unpublished memoir about her time with Kerouac. Excerpts from the latter are included in Brenda Knight's *Women of the Beat Generation* (Berkeley, CA: Conari Press, 1996).

Jan Kerouac

Though she only saw her father twice, Jack Kerouac's only child inherited his literary gifts and wanderlust. Jan Kerouac (1952–1996) had little formal schooling but developed her own distinct writing

Like father, like son . . . and daughter. William S. Burroughs published a first-person account of his heroin addiction—as Junkie *by "William Lee" in a 1953 paperback (since retitled* Junky*). He published the novel* Naked Lunch *in 1959 (titled* The Naked Lunch *in England, where this edition was published). His son, William Burroughs Jr., aka "Billy," published a first-person account of his own self-destructive addiction to amphetamines,* Speed *(1970). Jack Kerouac's only child, Jan Kerouac, published two well-received books that detailed her troubled childhood, hedonistic youth, and the wanderlust that she inherited from a father she only saw twice:* Baby Driver *(1981) and* Trainsong *(1988). (Courtesy of Tom Hearn.)*

style, with which she chronicled her life of hippie excess and adventure. Her friend Gerald Nicosia, who wrote the definitive biography of Jack Kerouac, said, "She was not writing because she was a famous man's daughter. She was writing because she had already lived far more broadly and intensely than most people, and because it was important to her to preserve as much of her life as possible in language."[1] Though she received some royalties from her father's work, Jan Kerouac battled his estate's executors over many things, including their sale of his image to Gap, to be used in an advertisement for khaki pants, and the sale of one of his raincoats to Johnny Depp. She also tried unsuccessfully to move her father's body from Lowell's Edson Cemetery to the family burial plot in Nashua, New Hampshire, where his father, mother, and brother were buried. She published two autobiographical novels, *Baby Driver* (1981) and *Trainsong* (1988). She died at age 44.

Note

1. Brenda Knight, *Women of the Beat Generation* (Berkeley, CA: Conari Press, 1996), 312.

Joan Haverty Kerouac

A dressmaker when she was dating Bill Cannastra (1931–1990), Haverty became a member of the early Beat circle in New York. After Cannastra was killed in a freakish subway accident, Kerouac began dating her; within two weeks they were married, in November 1950. By the spring of 1952 the couple had separated, but not before Kerouac had finished typing the "scroll" version of *On the Road* in their West 20th Street apartment and Joan had become pregnant. Their daughter, Jan Kerouac, was born in February 1952. Joan worked periodically over the years on an unpublished memoir about her and Kerouac, called *Nobody's Wife*. Excerpts from this work are included in Brenda Knight's *Women of the Beat Generation* (Berkeley, CA: Conari Press, 1996).

Liz Lehrman

Liz Lehrman (b. 1928), who later took the name Liza Williams, lived with Lucien Carr in New York after he was released from prison. She befriended Joan Haverty Kerouac, and went with the newly married couple to meet the Haverty family. Lehrman eventually moved to South Africa, married a musician, and became an antiapartheid activist. During the late 1960s, she lived in Los Angeles and was a widely read columnist for the *LA Free Press*, a hippie newspaper. Seven years of her journalism were compiled to make her book *Up the City of Angels* (1971).

Denise Levertov

Born in England, Denise Levertov (1923–1997) was educated at home and served as a civilian nurse in London during World War II. Her first book of poetry, *The Double Image* (1946), was praised for its "militant pacifism." She married an American writer, Mitchell Goodman, and moved to New York in 1948. Her poetry was influenced by the writings of William Carlos Williams, Wallace Stevens, and Charles Olson, and her friendships with Kenneth Rexroth, Robert Creeley, and Robert Duncan. She was considerably more "straight" than the rest of the Beat circle, but she stood her own ground and gained their respect. She taught at the University of California at Berkeley and was involved with both the antiwar and antinuclear movements.

Josephine Miles

An English professor at the University of California–Berkeley from 1940 until her death, Josephine Miles (1911–1985) was a vital member of the Bay Area literary scene that paved the way for the San Francisco Poetry Renaissance. In 1956, when Allen Ginsberg sought her out for graduate school advice, Miles, who was also an accomplished poet, was impressed with the young Beat. She introduced him to Richard Eberhart, who was working on an article for the *New York Times*. The resultant article, "West Coast Rhythms," which ran on September 2, 1956, brought national attention to the thriving poetry scene, and boosted the work of Kenneth Patchen, Kenneth Rexroth, City Lights Pocket Books, and Ginsberg.

Vickie Russell

Born Priscilla Arminger, Vickie Russell was the daughter of a Philadelphia judge. She entered the Beat circle through Herbert Huncke, with whom she traversed the underside of Manhattan. A striking redhead, Russell took up prostitution to make enough money to keep a steady supply of Benzedrine. Her boyfriend, Little Jack Melody, was a petty thief whose regular accomplice was Huncke. They hid their loot in Ginsberg's apartment. Ginsberg was arrested, along with Melody and Russell, when their stolen car was crashed and police searched Ginsberg's apartment to find the contraband. She befriended Joan Vollmer and often stayed at the communal apartment at 419 West 115th Street, along with Ginsberg, Burroughs, and Kerouac. She taught them how to purchase nasal inhalers, break them open and eat the Benzedrine-soaked cotton inside. This became a cheap staple for the Beats and helped fuel Kerouac's early writing binges.

Anne Waldman

Born in New Jersey in 1945 and raised in Greenwich Village, Anne Waldman was exposed to bohemian life at a young age. She idolized Gregory Corso, whom she saw on the streets of the city. "He was an idol in some sense," she told Ann Charters. "Like Rimbaud, he was the epitome of the 'damned' poet."[1] After graduating from Bennington College, Waldman moved to the Lower East Side in 1966. She started an influential magazine, *Angel Hair*, and was director of the Poetry Project at St. Mark's Church, which has become a staple of the New York arts scene since that time. She was a longtime member of the faculty, along with Allen Ginsberg and Diane di Prima, of the Jack Kerouac School of Disembodied Poetics at the Naropa Institute in Boulder, Colorado.

Note

1. "Introduction," in *The Portable Beat Reader*, ed. Ann Charters (New York: Viking, 1992), 427.

Appendix A: Beats on Screen, Served on Platters

Music

Describing jazz to television journalist Mike Wallace on *Night Beat* in January 1958, Kerouac said, "Jazz is the music of the Beat Generation. . . . It's just as complicated as Bach. The chords, the structures, the harmony. . . . And then it has a tremendous beat . . . a tremendous drive. It can drive you right out of yourself."[1] That, indeed, was what it did for Kerouac, who described jazz performances in his novels as if they were tent-revival faith-healing crusades. *Time* magazine in 1959 claimed that the "Beatniks' 3 Bs" were "Bach, Bartok and Bird."

In his groundbreaking 1957 essay "The White Negro," Norman Mailer credited jazz with opening the doors for "unconventional action" in America. "It is no accident that the source of Hip is the Negro for he has been living on the margin between totalitarianism and democracy for two centuries. But the presence of Hip as a working philosophy in the sub-worlds of American life is probably due to jazz, and its knife-like entrance into culture, its subtle but so penetrating influence on an avant-garde generation—that postwar generation of adventurers who had absorbed the lessons of disillusionment and disgust of the Twenties, the Depression, and the War." Further on, Mailer likened jazz to "orgasm." The music, he wrote, "spoke in no matter what laundered popular way of instantaneous existential states to which some whites could respond, it was indeed a communication by art because it said, 'I feel this, and now you do too.'"[2]

In *Collaborating with Kerouac*, David Amram related a story about Miles Davis that captured the essence of Beat jazz improvisation: "The band starts playing 'Bye Bye Blackbird' and Miles puts his trumpet down and turns his back to the audience for ten minutes. One guy turns to the other and says, 'Brother, I paid ten bucks to hear this cat blow his horn and he's strolling through the whole set. He ain't doing nothing. He hasn't played one note!' His friend turns to him and says, 'It's not what he's playing, it's what he's *thinking*.'"[3]

The bebop favored by Kerouac and many of the other Beats was a product of the 1940s and was characterized by wild improvisation, fast pace, loud volume, and often raucous spirit. In the 1950s, a new, more subdued and cerebral form of the music, dubbed "Cool Jazz" developed on the West Coast, the style described by musicologist Thomas Hine: "the tunes were usually succinct and accessible, and the innovations were more often formal experiments than personal explorations." Among the progenitors of this style were saxophonists Gerry Mulligan and Paul Desmond, and trumpeter Chet Baker. There was some overlap between the bebop and cool camps, in figures like Miles Davis and Art Pepper. Indeed, among the black jazz players who had the stamp of approval from the Beats were Davis and Pepper, as well as Charlie Parker, Bud Powell, Lester Young, Thelonious Monk, John Coltrane, Billie Holiday, Dizzy Gillespie (whose instrumental homage "Kerouac" was a staple of his live gigs), Lionel Hampton, Jimmie Lunceford, Jay McShann, Charles Mingus, Fats Navarro, Roy Eldridge, Count Basie, Max Roach, Dexter Gordon, Elvin Jones, Ornette Coleman, Slim Gaillard, and Babs Gonzalez. In addition, some white jazz musicians possessed the requisite unique style and flair that transcended their race, including Lenny Tristano, Chet Baker, Zoot Sims, Al Cohn (Sims and Cohn accompanied Kerouac on some of his recordings), Gerry Mulligan, Stan Getz, and George Shearing.

The music that the Beats loved matched their mood. As Jack Kerouac wrote in "The Origins of the Beat Generation," "The hipsters, whose music was bop, they looked like criminals, but they kept talking about the things I liked, long outlines of personal experience and vision, nightlong confessions full of hope that had become illicit and repressed by War, stirrings, rumblings of a new soul (that same old human soul). . . . By 1948 it began to take shape. That was a wild vibrating year when a group of us would walk down the street and yell hello and even stop and talk to anybody that gave us a friendly look."[4] And often, they were on their way to one of Manhattan's many jazz clubs to hear the bebop that they loved.

Rolling Stone compiled a list of "representative" recordings that contained the "bebop Kerouac, Cassady and their buddies were digging." Among these recordings were such classics as Miles Davis's *The Birth of the Cool* (1948–1950); Stan Getz's *Diz and Getz* (1953); Dizzy Gillespie's *Shaw 'Nuff* (1946); *Billie Holiday's Greatest Hits* (1944–1949); Jimmie Lunceford's *Swingsation* (1934–1938); Thelonious Monk's *Complete Blue Note Recordings* (1947–1957); and *Bird: The Complete Charlie Parker on Verve* (1946–1954).

Television

Peter Gunn (1958–1961)

Created by Blake Edwards, this weekly show aired on NBC and then ABC (114 episodes) and featured the titular private eye who hung

---

Jack Kerouac was stricken by his fatal stomach hemorrhage while watching *The Galloping Gourmet* on TV on October 21, 1969. He would die after nearly 30 blood transfusions in St. Anthony's Hospital in St. Petersburg, Florida. Kerouac's favorite bebop musician, Charlie Parker, also died while watching TV. Parker was watching the *Tommy Dorsey Show* at New York's Stanhope Hotel when he was stricken by a fatal bleeding ulcer.

out at a jazz club called Mother's, where his girlfriend performed as a sultry singer. The most distinctive feature was the use of contemporary Beat-flavored jazz in the soundtrack and the presence of beatnik habitués of Mother's.

The Many Loves of Dobie Gillis (1959–1963)

This television show featured the most famous Beatnik character in America. Portrayed by Bob Denver—who would later inhabit the hapless Gilligan character on *Gilligan's Island*—Maynard G. Krebs was the projection of all the stereotypes of the "Beatniks" in one person: goateed, lazy, irresponsible, muddled, disheveled in appearance, plays bongos, and sputters hipster lingo. However, Denver brought something poetic and subtle to his portrayal of Maynard G. Krebs ("the 'G' stands for Walter"—he was said to be named for his "Aunt Walter" who was married to his "Uncle Edith"). Because the series producers really did not know much about the Beats, Denver spent time in coffeehouses and jazz clubs, studying the Beatnik in his natural habitat. As a result, he brought some authenticity to the character of Maynard G. Krebs. Maynard

Beatniks were regular characters, usually comic relief, on many television shows of the late 1950s and early 1960s. They can be seen here, in episodes of The Danny Thomas Show *and* The Betty Hutton Show, *both on CBS-TV. (Courtesy of the New York World Telegram and Sun Collection, Library of Congress.)*

was, in fact, the most appealing character on a show that was otherwise populated by high-schoolers with the one-dimensionality of Archie Comics characters. Today, Maynard is the only character anyone remembers from the cast of *The Many Loves of Dobie Gillis*, which ran for four years on CBS.

One of the recurring motifs of the show was Maynard's studious avoidance of gainful employment. In fact, every time the word "work" was mentioned in conversation, he would jump back as if hit with a bullet and yelp, "Work?!" Reruns of the series have been a staple on the cable television network *Nick at Nite*. Denver, as Maynard G. Krebs, was said to have even recorded an album's worth of protest songs, called *Like, What?* by Maynard G. & the Krebs in 1961. The album turned out to be a hoax.

Staccato (1959–1960)

This weekly show aired on NBC and then ABC between September 1959 and March 1960 (27 episodes), starring John Cassevetes as Johnny Staccato, a New York private eye who also played jazz piano at a Greenwich Village bistro. Beatniks were regularly depicted on the show.

Route 66 (1960–1964)

This popular television series was created in the wake of the popularity of *On the Road*, and like Kerouac's novel featured two buddies wandering America's byways in search of "kicks" and adventure. (Contrary to the series title, very few episodes took place on or near U.S. Route 66.) According to biographer Dennis McNally, *Route 66* "sanitized *On the Road*" by "trading in a muddy 1949 Hudson for a gleaming Corvette Stingray . . . and taking the archetypal freedom image from Jack's book and adding George Maharis, an actor who eerily resembled Kerouac." Martin Milner played Maharis's clean-cut sidekick. Kerouac wanted to file a copyright infringement suit against series producer Stirling Silliphant but the lawyers he consulted told him there was insufficient evidence.

Movies

The Man with the Golden Arm (1955)

Based on Nelson Algren's controversial 1949 novel, this critically acclaimed film was directed by Otto Preminger and starred Frank Sinatra as a recovered heroin addict (a morphine addict in the book) and ex-convict who tried to make it outside of prison as a drummer for a jazz band. All of these themes were echoed in Beat literature—jazz, drugs, down and out, soul searching. Because it was successful—and was nominated for three Academy Awards—*The Man with the Golden Arm* forced the Motion Picture Association of America (MPAA) to revise its allowable subject matter to include formerly forbidden topics like drug addiction and prostitution. (The MPAA had refused to give the film its approval, due to its controversial topics.)

The Beat Generation (1959)

This film, produced by Hollywood veteran Albert Zugsmith, was quickly written, filmed, and released to take advantage of the Beatnik fad. And just as quickly forgotten. Though the movie posters claimed the film offered a glimpse "behind the weird way-out world of the Beatniks," biographer Dennis McNally called it "a sleazy B-grade opus of rape and assault." Zugsmith had copyrighted the title "The Beat Generation" to prevent Jack Kerouac, and others, from suing him. The soundtrack featured the decidedly un-Beatnik jazz great Louis Armstrong, and the cast featured Charlie Chaplin's son as the playboy-beatnik, Jackie Coogan (later Uncle Fester in *The Addams Family* TV series) as the "nutty" beatnik, Ray Danton as a rapist, Mamie Van Doren as the sex object, and a professional wrestling beatnik called "Slapsie Maxie."

Pull My Daisy (1959)

This quintessential Beat collaboration featured the talents and presence of major Beat-era figures across a wide spectrum of artistic genres, including art (Larry Rivers, Alice Neel, Alfred Leslie), photography (Robert Frank), music (David Amram), and literature (Jack Kerouac, Allen Ginsberg, Gregory Corso, Peter Orlovsky). Directed by Alfred Leslie, a rising star on the New York art scene, with camera work by Robert Frank, whose book *The Americans* (1958) was the most influential work of photography since the WPA photographers of the 1930s, *Pull My Daisy* featured the words and voice of Jack Kerouac. The screenplay was spontaneously written by Kerouac, adapted from a play that he had tentatively titled "The Beat Generation." He also did the voiceover for the footage of what otherwise was a silent film. David Amram's musical score, which played alongside Kerouac's voice, was composed in close collaboration with Kerouac. Amram also portrayed the character "Mezz McGillicuddy," a French horn player. Director Alfred Leslie gave all the players the instructions: "Be your delightful crazy anarchistic selves." His artistic summary statement was "Painters, poets, musicians, photographers, all capturing a moment of our joy together." The relatively short film (28 minutes) took an interminable amount of time to film because of the antics of the players, who drank wine, smoked pot, threw food, removed their clothes, improvised dances and gymnastic tricks (at one point, Corso leaped from the fire escape and chased a car down the Greenwich Village street outside Leslie's art studio, where the action was filmed). The only guidance they had was a three-page story outline by Kerouac. Through the chaos, the calm Leslie kept directing and Frank kept filming. The "plot" of the film, such as it was, was simple: Milo (Larry Rivers, a stand-in for Neal Cassady) returns home after a hard day of work as a railroad brakeman, to find his Beat friends (Ginsberg, Corso, Orlovsky, Amram) have made a shambles of his house while waiting for him to return. Milo's wife (played by the only professional actor in the cast, Delphine Seyrig) becomes furious at Milo's friends, especially after they pester the bishop and the bishop's wife (portrayed by famed bohemian artist Alice Neel) and daughter, who have come by for a visit. In the end, Milo's wife kicks them all out, but Milo goes with them. In a way, it was a microcosm of Neal and Carolyn Cassady's actual marriage.

In *Collaborating with Kerouac*, Amram described the day that Kerouac arrived at the studio to watch the filming: "The afternoon that Jack arrived, we celebrated even longer than usual before filming. Jack looked bemused as he studied the shambles of Alfred's [Leslie] usually immaculate studio. The floor was now strewn with crushed beer cans, soda pop bottles, and empty gallon jugs of red Gallo wine sticking to dried-up puddles spilled by their sides. Discarded wax paper wrappers from half-eaten pastrami sandwiches moved ever-so-slightly as hordes of cockroaches feasted on their greasy remains. Ground-up donuts, stale French fries covered in crusted ketchup that were now hard as rocks, were surrounded by scraps of paper with poems and sketches that had been torn up. Old underwear, towels, and socks that stood up by themselves had fallen from the broken-down chair. 'Good God, Alfred, my shoes are stuck to the floor,' said Jack. 'Neal's [Cassady] house never looked this bad. Carolyn wouldn't have allowed it.'

"'It's effective, though, to show why Delphine, who is playing Carolyn, becomes so furious that she throws everyone out at the end,' said Alfred. Jack slumped quietly in a chair, viewing the madhouse surroundings. It was 3:30 in the afternoon, and it seemed like midnight at a New Year's Eve party at a mental institution where the patients had taken over. Alfred came over and knelt by Jack's chair.

"'We have an excellent esprit de corps among our cast members,' Alfred said in a soothing voice.

"'So I've noticed,' said Jack."[5]

Jack Kerouac's narration was recorded a week after the filming was over. Leslie and Frank had edited down the hours of footage to a manageable length. While Amram played his piano composition, Kerouac intoned his narration in one long take. All of it was improvised, using the same three-page outline from which the actors had worked. When Kerouac was finished, Alfred Leslie said, "What you just did was beyond belief."

Amram recorded the score with a backing band comprised of Sahib Shihab on alto saxophone and Midhat Serbagi on viola, both of whom were fans of Kerouac. Sahib told Amram, "I wish Bird [Charlie Parker] had lived to get to read about himself in *On the*

Road. Kerouac is the only cat who understood where our music is coming from. . . . Jack was always cool. He's not white. He's not black. He's Kerouac."

Pull My Daisy went on to enjoy a long run at a Greenwich Village art cinema, but was never put into wide release nationwide. In 1996 the film was added to the National Film Registry at the Library of Congress. Kerouac would never again reach such a creative peak as during those weeks in Greenwich Village in early 1959.

The Beatniks (1960)

Written and directed by Paul Frees (best known as the "voice" of Boris Badenov in the Rocky and Bullwinkle cartoons), this exploitative film conflated the fear of juvenile delinquents with the "beatnik" stereotype. The film poster noted, "Exploding from alleyways and ivory towers. . . . The Beatniks living by their code of rebellion and mutiny!" Few more ridiculous films have ever been made.

The Subterraneans (1960)

Jack Kerouac was paid $15,000 for the rights to his short novel *The Subterraneans*, his single biggest payday. The plot and some of the characters of Kerouac's novel were dramatically altered, and the advertising tagline for the movie was, "These are The Subterraneans—Today's Young Rebels—who live and love in a world of their own. This is their story told to the hot rhythms of fabulous jazz!" The film's music was provided by legitimate Beat jazz figures Gerry Mulligan (who also portrayed "Reverend Joshua Hoskins," a character that wasn't in the novel), Shelly Manne, Red Mitchell, and Art Pepper, but it was somewhat undermined by André Previn's treacly orchestration. George Peppard portrayed Kerouac, Roddy McDowell portrayed Gregory Corso, Leslie Caron portrayed Mardou Fox, the mixed-race romantic lead, and Arte Johnson (later a mainstay on the *Laugh-In* TV show) portrayed a beatnik poet. The fictional beatnik bar that served as the setting for much of the action in the movie was called "Daddy's Catacombs," located in North Beach, San Francisco.

Greenwich Village Story (1963)

Written and directed by Jack O'Connell, this film used the later folk-music craze as the last gasp of the Beat Generation. Though somewhat inaccurate on that score, the film was, according to *Rolling Stone*, "the most affectionate, least clichéd of all the beatnik movies of that time . . . it closes the door on the real Beat world, and leaves all subsequent portrayals to be seen as ludicrous afterthoughts."[6]

Take Her, She's Mine (1963)

In this romantic comedy starring Jimmy Stewart and Sandra Dee, Bob Denver makes a memorable impression as "Emmett," the Beatnik singer at the Sleeping Pill Coffee House. The lyrics of his song comprise a parody of Allen Ginsberg's poem, "Howl": "Hopingly, pantingly, squallingly / Outwardly thrusting in pain and shock and disbelief . . . / Hopingly, graspingly, aspiringly . . . / Impermanently permanent / All interest canceled / Repossessed / Howl! Hooooowwwwwwllll!"

Heart Beat (1980)

Directed by John Byrum and based on a memoir by Carolyn Cassady, the wife of Neal Cassady, this film was the first serious attempt to examine the lives of the Beat principals. Nick Nolte portrayed Neal Cassady, Sissy Spacek played Carolyn Cassady, and John Heard portrayed Jack Kerouac. The result was far more suffocating and morbid than the actual events that inspired the memoir or the film.

Drugstore Cowboy (1989)

Written and directed by Gus Van Sant, based on a true-life novel by James Fogle, this feature film starred Matt Dillon and Kelly Lynch as itinerant drug addicts. It featured an appearance by Beat icon William

S. Burroughs as a defrocked priest who offers sage advice to the young addicts about the dangers of temptation. The film was critically acclaimed, as was Burroughs in his small part.

The Last Time I Committed Suicide (1997)

Written and directed by Stephen Kay and based on a letter written by Neal Cassady to Jack Kerouac, this critically acclaimed film reached only a small audience. At the time, 20-year-old Cassady (portrayed by Thomas Jane) was living in Denver and working the nightshift at a tire recapping plant. His letter, written in stream-of-consciousness and filled with wild digressions and linguistic improvisation, did in fact have an impact on Kerouac's writing style. The film builds on that same restless energy, portraying Cassady's legendary sexual prowess, while Adrien Brody portrays a homosexual who lusts after Cassady, based on the real-life dynamic that he had with poet Allen Ginsberg. Adding some real-life bohemian touches are actors Keanu Reeves and punk musician John Doe.

Neal Cassady (2008)

Written and directed by Noah Buschel, this biopic features Tate Donovan as Neal Cassady in a fairly authentic portrait of a conflicted man who found himself a legend and then tried to live up to that legend or die trying. Which he did (die, that is). Other actors include Amy Ryan as Carolyn Cassady, Glenn Fitzgerald as Jack Kerouac, and Chris Bauer as Ken Kesey.

Miscellaneous

Allen Ginsberg appeared in the opening sequence of D. A. Pennebaker's famous 1967 documentary about Bob Dylan, *Don't Look Back*. Ginsberg wanders through the scene in which the singer pantomimes "Subterranean Homesick Blues," a song that features Beat-influenced lyrics and an homage to Jack Kerouac's novel, *The Subterraneans*. Ginsberg helped write the cue cards that Dylan holds in this iconic sequence.

Francis Ford Coppola bought the film rights to Jack Kerouac's *On the Road* in 1968. Over forty years later, Coppola—director of *The Godfather* movies and *Apocalypse Now*—has yet to make the film. In 2002 he had tapped Joel Schumacher to direct and hired Russell Banks to write a screenplay. Banks did his job, but the film was not made.

Beatnik poets Lawrence Ferlinghetti and Michael McClure both appeared in The Band's farewell concert film, *The Last Waltz*, directed by Martin Scorsese.

Pop Culture

Beatnik themes, of a mostly satiric nature, appeared in pop music in such songs as "Beatnik Fly" and "Sugar Shack"; cartoons, in anthologies like *Beat Beat Beat* (edited by William Brown, a Princeton graduate who worked for the a Madison Avenue ad agency, Batten, Barton, Durstine & Osborn) and featured in *Mad* magazine and the comic strips *Pogo, Gordo,* and *Popeye* (to name a few). *Playboy* magazine featured a "Beat Playmate"; *Saturday Evening Post* featured a short story called "Beauty and the Beatnik"; the soap opera *Helen Trent* featured a Beatnik character; the 1959 Broadway musical, *The Nervous Set,* opened with the song, "Man, We're Beat" (and featured what would become a jazz standard, "Spring Can Really Hang You Up the Most"); "The Wildman of Wildsville" cartoon starred the characters Beany and Cecil, and featured the voices of real Beats like Lord Buckley and Scatman Crothers, and such lines as "if you can't beatnik 'em, join 'em" (before the song "Twinkle Twinkle Little Beatnik"); and the artist and designer Ed "Big Daddy" Roth built a car out of fiberglass in 1960, which became the famous Beatnik Bandit.

Notes

1. Dennis McNally, *Desolate Angel: Jack Kerouac, the Beat Generation, and America* (New York: Random House, 1979), 246–247.
2. Norman Mailer, "The White Negro," in *The Portable Beat Reader,* ed. Ann Charters (New York: Viking, 1992), 586–606.

3. David Amram, *Collaborating with Kerouac* (New York: Thunder's Mouth Press, 2002), 24.
4. Jack Kerouac, "The Origins of the Beat Generation," *Playboy*, June 1959.
5. Amram, *Collaborating with Kerouac*, 59–60.
6. Henry Cabot Beck, "From Beat to Beatnik," in *The Rolling Stone Book of the Beats: The Beat Generation and American Culture*, ed. Holly George-Warren (New York: Hyperion, 1999), 95–105.

Appendix B: Magazines That First Published Beat Generation Writers

The Beats. Editor Seymour Krim's paperback-only anthology popularized many of the Beat writers, who greeted it with suspicion when he proposed their contributing to it. Krim wrote, "To get the word out to the masses, and also to make a buck but not much more, I did the anthology The Beats, brought out by the hard-boiled adventure line of Gold Medal Books. . . . We went into two editions with the writers sharing the bread. Years later I would meet members of the hippie generation who said that this gaudily packaged parcel of what I believe was the real thing had stung their Texas or Ohio eyes like a can of Mace. I want to believe them." Krim also edited a "Beat Section" for a "girlie mag" called *Swank* and was an editor at the equally "tits-and-assed" *Nugget* from 1961 to 1965. Using this forum, which reached readers that would not be reached through "normal" channels, Krim was responsible for getting a wider audience for many writers who would later anchor the counterculture of the 1960s: Hubert Selby, Terry Southern, Norman Mailer, Frank O'Hara, Chandler Brossard and, of course, Ginsberg and Kerouac.[1]

Big Table. Edited by Paul Carroll, based in Chicago (Kerouac gave it the name). The first issue (Spring 1959) contained a 35-page prose poem by Kerouac called "Old Angel Midnight," three poems by

Gregory Corso, and "ten episodes from *Naked Lunch*" by William S. Burroughs. Oddly, the short biographical note about Burroughs mentions that he "is an expert marksman," even though eight years earlier he had accidentally killed his wife Joan while trying to shoot a glass off her head. Also, the first issue, 400 copies of *Big Table*, was impounded. An obscenity lawsuit, backed by the ACLU ensued, delaying the journal. Judge Julius Hoffman ruled in the magazine's favor and *Big Table* was served. Former *Big Table* editor Peter Michelson wrote, "*Big Table* helped give shape to the Beat and Black Mountain revolutions in poetics."

Black Mountain Review. Edited by Robert Creeley, who was wooed to teach at this North Carolina experimental college in order to also create their literary magazine. The autumn 1957 issue contained Ginsberg's now-famous poem "America," and an excerpt from Kerouac's lengthy spontaneous prose experiment, "October in the Railroad Earth." It also contained poems by Beat writers Philip Whalen, Michael McClure, and Gary Snyder, and an excerpt from William S. Burroughs's *Naked Lunch* (bylined "William Lee").

Chicago Review. Founded in 1946 and affiliated with the venerable University of Chicago, this review opened its pages to the Beats with its Spring 1958 issue. That issue contained a cover package headlined, "Ten San Francisco Poets" and included Ginsberg, Michael McClure, Philip Whalen, Lawrence Ferlinghetti, and Philip Lamantia, as well as Kerouac and Burroughs, though the latter two were better known as novelists. Kerouac also penned a short opening essay called "The Origins of Joy in Poetry," in which he wrote, "Poetry & prose had for a long time fallen into the false hands of the false. These new pure poets confess forth for the sheer joy of confession. . . . They SING, they SWING . . . SF is the poetry of a new Holy Lunacy like that of ancient times yet it also has that mental discipline typified by haiku, that is the discipline of pointing out things directly, purely, concretely, no abstractions or explanations, wham wham the true blue song of man." The Autumn 1958 issue contained an excerpt from *Naked Lunch* by William S. Burroughs, as well as work by Philip Whalen and Brother Antoninus. The issue came to the attention of conservative columnist Jack Mabley, who penned a vicious attack on the magazine and the university, which was reprinted on the front page of the *Chicago Daily News*, headlined, "Filthy Writing on the

Midway." Bowing to pressure, the university killed the Winter 1958 issue, which contained more work by Burroughs, Corso, and Kerouac. Four of the five editors at the *Review* resigned and created *Big Table*.

East Village Other. An irreverent arts and political biweekly cofounded by former *Village Voice* contributor John Wilcock, Walter Bowart, Allan Kurtzman, and Sherry Needham in 1965. Edited by Yaakov Kohn, a former member of the Israeli underground, the "EVO" was a transformational publication, which the *New York Times* called "so countercultural that it made the *Village Voice* look like a church circular." It served as a link between the Beats and the emerging hippie scene. The EVO, best known for its launching of underground comix artists like Spain Rodriguez, Kim Deitch, and Trina Robbins, ceased publication in 1972, but it influenced an entire generation of underground journalists.

Evergreen Review. Started in 1957 by Barney Rosset, the head of Grove Press, which also published many books by Beat writers. The print version of the magazine stopped publishing in 1973.

Kulchur. This New York–based magazine began publishing in 1960 and served as a venue for the second wave of Beat writers (LeRoi Jones, Denise Levertov, Diane di Prima, Hubert Selby, Ed Dorn, Frank O'Hara) and artists (Larry Rivers, Franz Kline), as well as some eclectic work by the major Beats, like an exchange of letters between Ginsberg and Burroughs. Editor Lita Hornick ceased publishing after 20 provocative and eclectic issues, now much coveted by collectors.

The Moderns. Edited by LeRoi Jones and published by Corinth Books in 1963, this was another hugely important, and wide selling, anthology that helped to popularize the work of Beat Generation writers and other outsiders from the academy. Among those included were neglected young writers like William Eastlake, Fielding Dawson, John Rechy, and Edward Dorn, as well as what were, by 1963, Beat writers who were gaining an audience, like Diane di Prima, William Burroughs, Robert Creeley, and Jack Kerouac. In his introduction to the volume, Jones wrote, "I am not interested in building another 'establishment' but only in gathering together an intelligent body of work that is separate from the one that exists."

The New American Poetry. Prior to the publication of this anthology, edited by Donald Allen and published by Evergreen Books/

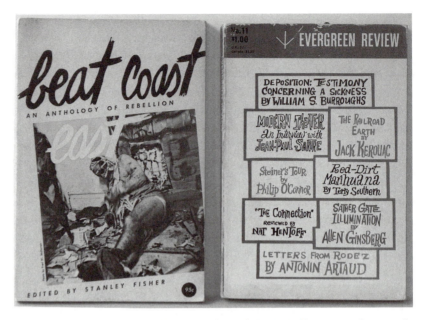

Simultaneous with the popularizing of novels by Jack Kerouac and poetry by Allen Ginsberg were the appearances of anthologies and periodicals where Beatnik writing found a home. The best known was Evergreen Review, *started in 1957 by Grove Press publisher Barney Rosset, which published some of Kerouac's finest short works, like "The Railroad Earth" in this issue (January/February 1960), and "Essentials of Spontaneous Prose" (Summer 1958).* Beat Coast East *was an anthology compiled by the New York artist Stanley Fisher in 1960. (Courtesy of Tom Hearn.)*

Grove Press in 1960, the standard "canon" in the university world was represented by *Norton Anthology of Modern Poetry* and the *New Poets of England and America*, edited by Louis Simpson, Donald Hall, and Robert Pack. The latter was published in 1957 and it was that anthology that Allen's anthology met head-on, in what came to be known as the "Battle of the Anthologies" (see below) Theirs was a clearly delineated view of what was "acceptable" in poetry and the literary fortress was guarded by severe and venerable critics like T. S. Eliot, F. R. Leavis, Cleanth Brooks, and Robert Penn Warren. Allen's anthology, along with *Evergreen Review, New World Writing,* and Krim's *The Beats,* stormed the moat and the portcullis of the academy, bringing begrudging respect to the work of the Beats and many other writers who, though not affiliated with them, were unorthodox or unfairly ignored through lack of scholarly champions. This anthology, which went into numerous printings and is still in print, contained work by writers either directly or indirectly affiliated with the Beats (Brother Antoninus, Ray Bremser, Corso, Creeley, Duncan, Ferlinghetti, Ginsberg, Jones, Kerouac, Lamantia, Levertov, McClure, Olson, Orlovsky, Snyder, Spicer, and Welch, Whalen).

New World Writing. This prestigious anthology began in 1952 as a paperback-only volume published by New American Library, dedicated to "introducing new writers, publishing exciting new work by established writers, and maintaining a consistently high literary standard." When the Beat writers began appearing in *New World Writing* (e.g., Kerouac's "Jazz of the Beat Generation," published in *New World Writing* 7 [April 1955]), they had cleared a major hurdle. After helping to break some of the Beat writers of the 1950s, *New World Writing* No. 16, in 1960, published the first piece by Thomas Pynchon, who became a dominant American writer in the following decades.

Providence Review. Edited by William V. Ward and Harriet Sohmers, this journal published six issues between 1958 and 1963, most of which included work by Beat writers. Editor Ward was arrested for "publishing obscene literature and selling it to minors" when Hubert Selby Jr.'s "Tralala" appeared in one of the issues.[2]

The Village Voice. Cofounded by Norman Mailer, Daniel Wolf, and Ed Fancher in 1955, the *Village Voice* was a vital supporter of the avant-garde and underground art, poetry, drama, and music scenes in New York. Staff writers like Mailer, Bill Manville, Jerry Tallmer, David McReynolds, Seymour Krim, and John Wilcock were predisposed to be supportive of the Beats, and picture editor Fred McDarrah was the most active chronicler of the Beat scene. He also started a "Rent-A-Beatnik" business.

Yugen. Started by LeRoi Jones (later Imamu Amiri Baraka) and his wife Hettie Jones in 1958, along with Totem Press, both in New York. The magazine was important for being an early supporter of Beat and Black Mountain College writers, setting the table, so to speak, for other larger magazines like *Evergreen Review* to carry them. Ray Bremser, Corso, Kerouac, Ginsberg, Frank O'Hara,

Charles Olson, Joel Oppenheimer, Gary Snyder, John Wieners, and Philip Whalen were published in this magazine. Totem Press also published books of poetry by Diane di Prima, Philip Whalen, Gary Snyder, Michael McClure, Gregory Corso, Allen Ginsberg, and Jack Kerouac. LeRoi Jones's own *Preface to a Twenty Volume Suicide Note* was an essential book of Beat verse. Jones told an interviewer in 1960, "I didn't especially think that there was any charted-out area in which the poetic sensibility had to function to make a poem."[3]

In 1996 Allen Ginsberg spoke to the author about these anthologies and the sorts of obstacles that stood in their way to mainstream acceptance.

Q: Speaking of San Francisco, according to my *Literary Companion* calendar, yesterday was the 41st anniversary of your first public reading of "Howl," at the Six Gallery there. That reading has become a sort of symbol of throwing down the gauntlet at the feet of the academy. At least, it seems to have come in hindsight to represent that . . .
Ginsberg: No, it was intentional then, because we were all influenced by William Carlos Williams, who had been rejected by the academic anthologies. The only thing they had around was his poem "The Yachts," which they repeated over and over again, but none of his later work and none of his early interesting work, and none of his companions of the Objectivist and activist movement were in the anthologies. By that I mean, specifically, Lorine Niedecker, Mina Loy, Louis Zukofsky, Charles Olson, Karl Rakosi, and Charles Reznikoff. So, when you opened one of the regular standard anthologies, you get Whitman as the representative of free verse, and Pound and Eliot as the cut up and montage guys, a little specimen of William Carlos Williams, and then you go back to John Crowe Ransom and Robert Penn Warren and all the academic poets. Robert Lowell and Donald Hall and Louis Simpson and John Hollander and Richard Howard and blah blah blah. But the whole world of Frank O'Hara, Kenneth Koch, John Ashbery, Robert Creeley, Charles Olson and their inheritors was eliminated, as well as Kerouac as a poet, myself as a poet, Gregory Corso. So, in 1957, I came back to New York with manuscripts of Olson, Creeley, Kerouac, myself, Corso, Denise Levertov, O'Hara and whatnot, and I brought it all to Louis Simpson. He was putting together

the Hall-Simpson-Pack anthology called *New Poets of England and America*. And between Pack, Simpson and Hall, they rejected every single one of these poets, who are now big poetic figures and heroes. So Donald Allen at Grove Press, who was gay, and was friends with O'Hara and me and Baraka, put together his anthology called *The New American Poetry*. Both of those books came out the same year, 1960, and there was no crossover. Actually, though, in real life there was some crossover, because Robert Lowell had been learning from Williams, and it had changed his whole style and been veering toward a more open form than before. So, in those days, that became known as "The Battle of the Anthologies." And now almost every one of those poets, except a very few who write a very strict form like William Jay Smith and Richard Wilbur—who are both really good at what they do—almost every one of them have opened up, like Donald Hall, and found their own stiff form of free verse [laughs]. Well, freer verse.

Notes

1. Elliott Anderson and Mary Kinzie, eds., *The Little Magazine in America: A Modern Documentary History* (Yonkers, NY: Pushcart Press, 1978), 334–335.
2. Fred McDarrah and Timothy McDarrah, *Kerouac and Friends: A Beat Generation Album* (New York: Thunder's Mouth, 2002), 246.
3. Anderson and Kinzie, *The Little Magazine in America*, 320.

Appendix C: Beat Jokes and Cartoons

The Beatnik became a staple of humor for the mainstream culture. Bob Hope, Betty Hutton, Danny Thomas, and many other comedians and comic actors took jabs at the stereotype, mostly playing off the idea that Beatniks were shiftless, lazy, nutty eggheads. Indeed, "egghead" became something of a pejorative in the 1950s, a term that was used even to undermine the two presidential campaigns of Senator Adlai Stevenson, a thoroughly decent man and one of the smartest politicians the nation has ever seen. An audience was ready-made in America for any commodities that took these sorts of "smarty pants" down a notch.

"Beatniks" found themselves most often satirized in bestselling mass-market paperback books. For example, in *Beat Jokes, Bop Humor, and Cool Cartoons* by Robert G. Reisner, with cartoons by Cecil Brathwaite (Citadel Press, 1960), one cartoon shows a pair of gad-about Beatniks on a trip to Paris (going to Paris was itself considered "egghead" behavior). One of the Beatniks leans down to talk to a local boy and then turns to his friend to inform him, "Man, even the kids here speak French." Another cartoon shows a Beatnik at a rehearsal for a production of Shakespeare's *Hamlet*. The caption has him saying, "Like to be or not to be."

Those who couldn't join the Beatniks took refuge in ridiculing them. Beat Beat Beat *(Signet, 1959) was a typical collection of "cool cartoons" that mocked Beatniks. (Courtesy of Tom Hearn.)*

Even life-threatening scenarios involving Beatniks were considered a source of great mirth. In *A Beat Generation Joke Book*, for example, a cartoon shows a drowning beatnik who is trying to get the lifeguard's attention. "Like help!" he screams. The alleged predilection for drugs was another source of "beatnik humor." In *Beat Beat Beat: A Hip Collection of Cool Cartoons about Life and Love among the Beatniks* by William F. Brown (Signet Books, 1959), a beatnik boy sits on Santa Claus's lap, demanding of the fat and friendly man: "I want a fix." Also, two beatniks discussing religion over coffee: "Well, if Billy Graham chooses to ignore Zen, Zen chooses to ignore Billy Graham."

The most lucrative riff on the Beatnik phenomenon was to show how most of the followers of this trend were really just phonies or, eventually, sellouts. Indeed, a series of cartoons in *Beat Beat Beat* follows the transformation of a young man. In the first one, he says, "Way back, man, I used to whiff a little of the pod . . . keep up with the cool cats in high school . . ."; (2) "Later it was motorcycles, hotrods, chicken runs, Brando movies"; (3) "Then I really balled with that New Orleans jazz . . ."; (4) "Finally I was flying high, Zen Buddhism, yab-yum sessions, rucksack wanderings with kindred souls . . ."; (5) "But one night, in the Village, I met this vessel from Wellesley. . ."; (6) "I began to look upon my former life as a kind of conformity. . ."; (7) "her old man set me up down at Amalgamated Tool & Die . . ."; (8) "I found out I liked Westport, PTA, TV and tailfins!" The final frame shows the man, dressed like a corporate commuter, a tormented look on his face as he says, "My psychiatrist tells me I'm a happy man."

Misery loves company, even in the mainstream.

Appendix D: Precursors to the Beats

The following cultural figures have been cited by members of the "Beat Generation" as having had an influence upon them:

Nelson Algren (1909–1981): American novelist (*A Walk on the Wild Side*, *The Man with the Golden Arm*).

James Baldwin (1924–1987): American expatriate novelist (*Go Tell It on the Mountain*).

Djuna Barnes (1892–1982): American novelist and bohemian best known for *Nightwood* (1936), which William Burroughs called "one of the great books of the 20th century."

Charles Baudelaire (1821–1867): French writer known for 1857 work *Les Fleurs du mal* (*Flowers of Evil*).

William Blake (1757–1827): Visionary English poet-artist who inspired Allen Ginsberg.

Maxwell Bodenheim (1896–1954): American bohemian poet and novelist.

Paul Bowles (1910–1999): Expatriate American novelist and composer who lived for 50 years in Morocco, where he proved helpful to William Burroughs.

Louis-Ferdinand Celine (1894–1961): French writer best known for his controversial novels (*Journey to the End of the Night*, *Death on the Installment Plan*).

Paul Cezanne (1839–1906): French painter who pointed the way to modernism.

Samuel Taylor Coleridge (1772–1834): English poet renowned for his opium-fueled poem "Kubla Khan."

Colette (pen name of Sidonie Gabrielle Claudine Colette de Jouvenel) (1873–1954): French novelist.

Hart Crane (1899–1932): Tormented American poet best known for *The Bridge* (1930).

e. e. (Edward Estlin) cummings (1894–1962): American poet and painter.

Thomas DeQuincey (1785–1859): British writer best known for *Confessions of an English Opium-Eater* (1821), an account that shaped William Burroughs's drug writings.

H. D. (Hilda Doolittle) (1886–1961): American bohemian poet.

Fyodor Dostoyevsky (1821–1881): Russian novelists whose works *Notes from Underground* and *The Idiot* deeply touched the Beats.

Marcel Duchamp (1887–1968): French expatriate artist, Dadaist and philosopher.

Kenneth Fearing (1902–1961): American bohemian poet.

Federico Garcia Lorca (1899–1936): Spanish poet and activist.

André Gide (1869–1951): French novelist.

Joe Gould (1889–1957): Street philosopher, poet, and "oral historian" who held forth in Manhattan barrooms.

Woody Guthrie (1912–1967): American musical legend and writer (*Bound for Glory*).

Aldous Huxley (1894–1963): British expatriate novelist and essayist whose tracts on psychedelic drugs, *Heaven and Hell* and *The Doors of Perception*, influenced the Beats.

Robinson Jeffers (1887–1962): American poet who wrote extensively about nature and the unspoiled area around Big Sur in California.

James Joyce (1882–1941): Irish novelist whose *Ulysses* (1922) expanded the possibilities of language as well as challenged America's obscenity laws.

Weldon Kees (1914–1955): San Francisco writer who organized pre-Beat artistic events.

D. H. Lawrence (1885–1930): British novelist whose *Lady Chatterley's Lover* (1928) challenged American obscenity laws.

Jack London (1876–1916): American novelist and journalist whose "road" narratives influenced Jack Kerouac.

Norman Mailer (1923–2007): American novelist and essayist.

Herman Melville (1819–1891): American novelist whose works "Bartleby the Scrivener" and *Moby Dick* deeply influenced Kerouac, Charles Olson, and other Beats writers.

Thomas Merton (1915–1968): American poet, spiritual writer, Trappist monk whose efforts to bridge East and West found a receptive audience among the Beats.

Henry Miller (1891–1980): American expatriate novelist whose *Tropic of Cancer* (1934) opened doors to previous forbidden subject matter and language.

Anaïs Nin (1903–1977): Cuban-French diarist and novelist whose confessional writings were touchstones to many women Beat writers.

Charles Olson (1910–1970): American poet, Melville authority, Black Mountain teacher.

Kenneth Patchen (1911–1972): American poet and painter who performed his work to jazz accompaniment.

Edgar Allan Poe (1809–1849): American short story master and visionary poet.

Marcel Proust (1871–1922): French novelist whose multivolume legend *Remembrances of Things Past* was an inspiration for Kerouac's Duluoz Legend.

John Reed (1893–1920): American bohemian poet, journalist, and revolutionary.

Arthur Rimbaud (1854–1891): French poet.

J. D. Salinger (b. 1919): American writer best known for *The Catcher in the Rye* (1951).

William Saroyan (1908–1981): American novelist.

Harry Smith (1923–1991): American folk music archivist and bohemian artist.

D. T. Suzuki (1870–1960): Japanese translator and scholar of Buddhism.

Dylan Thomas (1914–1963): Welsh poet.

Paul Verlaine (1844–1896): French poet.

Alan Watts (1915–1973): British expatriate writer and Zen authority who lived in the San Francisco Bay Area.

Walt Whitman (1819–1892): American poet whose lifelong work was *Leaves of Grass*.

William Carlos Williams (1883–1963): American poet and Ginsberg champion.

Thomas Wolfe (1900–1938): American novelist whose *Look Homeward, Angel* (1929) influenced Jack Kerouac's first novel, *The Town and the City*.

Louis Zukofsky (1904–1978): American poet.

Appendix E: The Beat Progeny

Caleb Carr, the best-selling novelist (*The Alienist*), is the son of Lucien Carr, who was a friend of Jack Kerouac, William Burroughs, and Allen Ginsberg and a key member of the Beat Generation circle. Another son, Simon Carr, is a successful painter.

Robert De Niro, the actor, is the son of Robert De Niro Sr., an abstract expressionist painter who was a member of the Beat circle in New York.

Bruce Fearing, a minor Beat poet, was the son of Kenneth Fearing, a renowned bohemian poet of the 1920s and 1930s and novelist (*The Big Clock*).

Neal and Carolyn Cassady had three children; they named their youngest John Allen Cassady, in honor of both Jack Kerouac and Allen Ginsberg.

Jack Kerouac and William S. Burroughs both had children who became writers. Burroughs's son, William S. Burroughs Jr., wrote two "autobiographical novels," *Speed* (1970) and *Kentucky Ham* (1973). Kerouac's daughter, Jan, wrote similar books entitled *Baby Driver* (1981) and *Trainsong* (1988).

Jack Kerouac met his daughter Janet Michelle "Jan" Kerouac (born February 16, 1952) for the first time when she was 16. She tracked him down to a bar in Lowell, Massachusetts, and he gave her his blessing to use the family name.

Writer Daniel Pinchbeck is the son of Joyce Johnson, whose relationship with Jack Kerouac is chronicled in the award-winning *Minor Characters* (1983).

Glossary

Much of the lingo of the Beats derived from the patois of the American jazz scene, with a few added twists peculiar to the 1950s. Among the people who helped shape and disseminate that lingo were standup comics Lenny Bruce and Mort Sahl, monologist Richard "Lord" Buckley, jazz musicians Slim Gaillard and Babs Gonzalez, and Chicago deejay Ken Nordine. While none of these people considered themselves "Beats," per se, their influence on "Beatniks" was undeniable, offering new ideas, new ways of speaking, new vocabularies, even new ways of walking and dressing.

Like these entertainers, Jack Kerouac was fond of inventing his own words or combinations of words. A typical Kerouac riff, from *On the Road*, was "peotl grooking in the desert to eat our hearts alive." In "Old Angel Midnight," his first long piece of "spontaneous prose," Kerouac coined words like "mesaroolies," "twandow," "dronk," "wartfence," "fradilaboodala," and so on, for 30 pages. Neal Cassady also added his lingo to the mix, the product of the pool halls and bars of Denver, where he was raised. Cassady used expressions like "bangtail," "booble," "kicks," and "blasted" (which meant smoking marijuana, which he called "t"). Cassady was also known as the "Holy Goof," hung on him by Kerouac in *On the Road*. One of Allen Ginsberg's

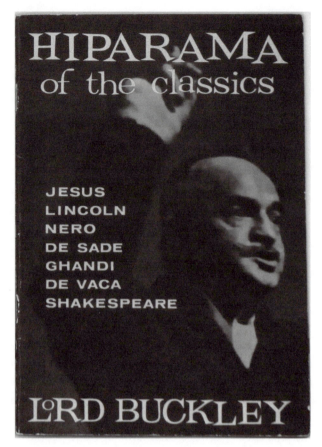

Lord Buckley became such a beacon of inspiration for the Beat Generation that Lawrence Ferlinghetti—who acknowledged Buckley's influence on his poetry—published a booklet of his routines through his City Lights imprint, Hiparama of the Classics. *Jack Kerouac was said to quote from Buckley's routines from memory. (Courtesy of Tom Hearn.)*

favorite coined words was "ignu," which he defined alternately as "an angel in comical form" and a "special honorary type post hip intellectual." He also, along with Kerouac, used "Holy" as an all-purpose exclamation of religious ecstasy and referred to fellow Beat searchers as "angel-headed." William S. Burroughs and Herbert Huncke introduced the parlance of the drug world to the mainstream, such words as "works," for syringe and spoon needed to shoot heroin; "shake" for drug raid; "joy bang" for occasional, nonaddictive use of heroin; and "hot shot," a toxic dose of heroin sold to junkies who are informers.

One of Kerouac's New York friends, the black poet Ted Joans, was famous for hosting readings in Greenwich Village venues like Café Rienzi (above which he lived), Café Bizarre, and the Gaslight. At these, he often recited his "jazz poem" called "The Sermon," which opened, "So you want to be hip, little girls? And you want to learn to swing? And you want to be able to dig and take in everything?" A former trumpet player, Joans had a feel for improvisation, and he coined many new phrases that made the rounds of the hip. He created what he called "giggly labels" like chicklets (younger than chicks), hipnicks, flipnicks, touristniks, jivey leaguer, creepnik, A-Trainer (Black men who took the A-Train from Harlem to Greenwich Village in search of White chicks), Bronx Bagel Babies, and the ultimate, the hipstressnik.

The word "Beat" itself was an invention, or an expropriation of an existing word for a different purpose. Later, most of the Beat glossary was adopted and adapted, with very little alterations, by the hippies in the 1960s and the punks in the 1970s. Lawrence Lipton in *The Holy Barbarians* (1959) compiled a list of "Beat" terms, based on his intimate connection to the scene. Lipton, a poet and journalist who went on to write for the *Los Angeles Free Press* during the hippie years, recorded his own album of jazz-accompanied poetry, *Jazz Canto: Volume I* (there was no Volume II). Among the terms that Lipton found to be conversational staples of the Beatnik in the 1950s were:

ax: Musical instrument.

bread: Money (e.g., "Could you lay some bread on me?").

bugged: Bothered, bedeviled, unstrung.

cat: The swinging, sex-free, footloose, nocturnal, uninhibited, nonconformist genus of the human race.

cool: Said of anything that sends you, whether cool jazz or a cool chick.

crazy: Anything from mild to wild that meets with a cat's approval. "Dig that crazy short." ("Short" was, in turn, defined as "a small foreign sports car.")

dig: To fully understand and appreciate.

drag: A boring situation. Lipton noted, "An evening with squares is a sad drag."

gone: Lipton wrote, "if you go far out enough you're gone." A famous Beatnik joke at the time went: "A beatnik asks the waitress for a piece of apple pie. The waitress says, 'Sorry, the apple pie is gone.' 'Oh man,' the beatnik responds excitedly. 'In that case, I'll take two pieces!'"

groove: To exult or bask in. Beatniks were using variations on this, like "groovey," long before the hippies adopted the term. (Or, as Lipton noted in 1959, "A hip chick is a groovey chick.")

hipster: An in-the-know person. "A cool cat." (Norman Mailer, in his essay "The White Negro," makes the case that the hipster predated the Beatnik.)

hype: Heroin user (short for "hypodermic").

like: An all-purpose word that has since never gone out of style. Lipton noted, "The theory of relativity applied to reality. 'Like that's your reality, man.'"

pad: Home or apartment.

split: Taking one's leave.

swinging: Uninhibited; the opposite of uptight or "hung up."

turn on: To introduce somebody to something new, as in, "He turned me on to Zen Buddhism."

wig: To be driven mad, as "flip your wig" or "wig out."

with it: In the know. It went without saying that a Beatnik was "with it."

wow: An all-purpose Beatnik word, like "like."

Note

1. William Brown, *Beat Beat Beat* (New York: Signet, 1959).

Primary Documents

Many of the writers, performers, and artists associated with the Beats and Beatniks are known for phrases or statements or entire passages that, through repetition, recitation, and reuse in other venues have become culturally iconic. The most often quoted are the originators of the Beat Generation.

Words of the Beats

1. William S. Burroughs

One morning in April, I woke up a little sick. I lay there looking at shadows on the white plaster ceiling. I remembered a long time ago when I lay in bed beside my mother, watching lights from the street move across the ceiling and down the walls. I felt the sharp nostalgia of train whistles, piano music down a city street, burning leaves. A mild degree of junk sickness always brought me the magic of childhood.

—opening of *Junky*

I can feel the heat closing in, feel them out there making their moves, setting up their devil doll stool pigeons.

—opening of *Naked Lunch*

2. Neal Cassady

What's your road, man? Holyboy road, madman road, rainbow road, guppy road, any road. It's an anywhere road for anybody anyhow.

—attributed to the fictional Dean Moriarty in *On the Road*

To have seen a specter isn't everything, and there are death-masks piled, one atop the other, clear to heaven.

—from "Joan Anderson letter" to Jack Kerouac, December 1950

For a time, I held a unique position: among the hundreds of isolated creatures who haunted the streets of lower downtown Denver, there was not one so young as myself.... Being thus grafted onto them, I became the unnatural son of a few score beaten men.

—opening of *The First Third*, an unfinished autobiography, published posthumously

3. Gregory Corso

Should I get married? Should I be good? / Astound the girl next door / with my velvet suit and faustus hood?

—opening lines of "Marriage"

Budger of history Brake of time You Bomb / Toy of universe Grandest of all snatched-sky / I cannot hate you.

—opening lines of "Bomb"

4. Allen Ginsberg

I have seen the best minds of my generation destroyed by madness starving hysterical naked, / dragging themselves through the negro streets at dawn looking for an angry fix, / angelheaded hipsters burning for the ancient heaveny connection to the starry dynamo in the machinery of night.

—opening lines of "Howl"

My wrath must end. All my images now are of heaven.... In the hospital I hope to be cured. My images tell me that the hours of truth are at hand.... I have been reading [Dostoevsky's] *The Possessed*. My devils have been cast out.

—journal entry, June 28, 1949, from *The Book of Martyrdom and Artifice: First Journals and Poems, 1937–1952*, edited by Juanita Lieberman-Plimpton and Bill Morgan

Are you going to let your emotional life be run by Time Magazine?
—from the poem "America"

Interview

In the 1950s, as one of the movers and shakers of the Beat Generation, Allen Ginsberg (1926–1997) saw the best minds of his generation sabotaged by madness, materialism, and American manifest destiny. His poem "Howl," published in the book *Howl and Other Poems* (1956) was, in fact, the Beat gauntlet hurled at the feet of America's literary academy as he and kindred spirits Jack Kerouac, William Burroughs, Carl Solomon (to whom the poem was dedicated), Neal Cassady, and Gregory Corso descended into the maelstrom ("What sphynx of cement and aluminum bashed open their skulls and ate up their brains and imagination?"). The spirit of that seminal work was picked up by succeeding generations of disaffiliated youth—mods, hippies, punks—each learning the painful lesson that the maelstrom never ended. The interview was conducted by Alan Bisbort in October 1996. Ginsberg died in April 1997.

Q: I'm interested in speaking to you about your new recording, "Ballad of the Skeletons," and your new book, *Selected Poems*, but, if it's okay, I'd first like to backtrack and talk about your role as celebrator of a literature that is really an antidote to the academy. The real face of literature, if you will. Do you think that's a fair characterization?
AG: Yes, up to a point. But if you want to be a bit more precise in your definition of the academy, it would be the kind of verse form and subject matter and diction that was featured in the standard anthologies—published by Norton and Macmillan and others—until

1950 or 1955. This did not include very much of William Carlos Williams or Ezra Pound. It completely ignored Karl Rakoski or Charles Reznikoff or Marsden Hartley or free form poetry of any form.

Q: I wasn't aware that [the American painter] Marsden Hartley wrote poetry.

AG: He was a great poet. A beautiful book of his poems was published by Black Sun and I came across it through William Carlos Williams. I asked him in 1950 what other poets wrote in the open form, and he recommended Hartley. And boy, I really was amazed. I went to the Gotham Book Market and found that book.

Q: Here's another one to throw at you from left field. Are you familiar of the early poems of Kenneth Fearing? In the late 1920s, he wrote wonderful books of poetry that were pigeon-holed as "proletarian" verse, but the voice in them is like someone screaming in the wilderness, a forerunner of the Beats.

AG: I may not be familiar with his early poems. Was that in the 1920s or 1930s?

Q: He published his first book in the mid-1920s as a pillar of the Greenwich Village bohemian scene ... one journalist called him as the personification of the "drunken poet."

AG: The early ones I may not know. But I knew Fearing. He was around San Francisco when I arrived. We met and were both interested in the same things. He loaned me his copy of Blaise Cendrars's *Voyage* published by Black Sun, translated by John Dos Passos. In those days, that was a very rare book, anything on Harry Crosby's old press was rare. But he loaned it to me and let me take it home for a couple of weeks. It was such a generous thing to do.

Q: Speaking of San Francisco, according to my *Literary Companion* calendar, yesterday was the anniversary of your first public reading of "Howl," at the Six Gallery there. That reading has become a sort of symbol of throwing down the gauntlet at the feet of the academy. At least, it seems to have come in hindsight to represent that....

AG: No, it was intentional then, because we were all influenced by William Carlos Williams, who had been rejected by the academic anthologies. The only thing they had around was his poem "The Yachts," which they repeated over and over again, but none of his later work and none of his early interesting work, and none of his companions of the Objectivist and activist movement were in the anthologies. By that I mean, specifically, Lorine Niedecker, Mina Loy, Louis Zukofsky, Charles Olson, Karl Rakosi, and Charles Reznikoff. So, when you opened one of the regular standard anthologies, you get Whitman as the representative of free verse, and Pound and Eliot as the cut up and montage guys, a little specimen of William Carlos Williams, and then you go back to John Crowe Ransom and Robert Penn Warren and all the academic poets. Robert Lowell and Donald Hall and Louis Simpson and John Hollander and Richard Howard and blah blah blah. But the whole world of Frank O'Hara, Kenneth Koch, John Ashbery, Robert Creeley, Charles Olson, and their inheritors was eliminated, as well as Kerouac as a poet, myself as a poet, Gregory Corso.

So, in 1957, I came back to New York with manuscripts of Olson, Creeley, Kerouac, myself, Corso, Denise Levertov, O'Hara, and whatnot, and I brought it all to Louis Simpson. He was putting together the Hall-Simpson-Pack anthology called *New Poets of England and America*. And between Pack, Simpson, and Hall, they rejected every single one of these poets, who are now big poetic figures and heroes. So Donald Allen at Grove Press, who was gay, and was friends with O'Hara and me and Baraka, put together his anthology called *The New American Poetry*. Both of those books came out the same year, 1960, and there was no crossover. Actually, though, in real life there was some crossover, because Robert Lowell had been learning from Williams, and it had changed his whole style and been veering toward a more open form than before. So, in those days, that became known as "The Battle of the Anthologies." And now almost every one of those poets, except a very few who write a very strict form like William Jay Smith and Richard Wilbur—who are both really good at what they do—almost every one of them have opened up, like Donald Hall, and found their own stiff form of free verse [laughs]. Well, freer verse.

Q: I've spoken with Ann Charters up here at University of Connecticut about her work with the Kerouac *Letters* and the *Beat Reader*.

AG: She was at Berkeley when I did my second "Howl" reading. At the first reading, I just did the first part of "Howl," but at Berkeley a few months later, in March 1956, I read not only a complete "Howl" (with Parts 2 and 3, which I hadn't read the first time), but also "Sun-flower Sutra" and "America." And she was at that reading as Peter Orlovsky's date ... isn't that crazy? And it was at that reading that she met her future husband Sam [Charters]. That was a real historic moment in her personal life ... isn't it funny that she was Peter's date? Because he always had girls....

Q: She has kindled the flame of beat literature since the mid-1960s.

AG: The first thing that really got her into it was doing a bibliog-raphy of Jack Kerouac's work. The reason she was so much onto it was that she and her husband knew a lot about jazz and bebop and folk music and American language from the point of view of black song. In fact, she had already put on a performance of *Treemonisha*, an opera written by Scott Joplin in 1911 ... she'd recorded it. She was recording Scott Joplin's rags before Joplin was revived in the 1960s.

Q: This leads to my next question, about your own music. I noticed that Ann Charters was credited with producing the first ver-sion of *First Blues*, the album later released in 1981.

AG: Yes and no. That was a Folkways record, called *First Blues*. It has a very interesting lineage. It was recorded by the great archivist Harry Smith. In 1952 Harry Smith put out a three-box, six-record set of American folk music through Folkways Records that influ-enced Dylan, influenced Jerry Garcia, influenced the folk music in general. It revived folk music in the early 1950s. Peter, Paul & Mary learned everything they knew from that, and Dylan learned from that. Harry Smith got to be a friend of mine in 1960. We met at a series of evenings with Thelonious Monk at the Five Star. Then at one point Harry stayed with me, because he was indigent. When he was living at the Chelsea Hotel he was doing a series of recordings called "Materials for the Study of Religion and Culture on the Lower East Side." He recorded jump-rope rhymes, kids' rhymes, rapping, Rasta talk, all of Gregory Corso's early poetry, all of Peter Orlovsky's early poetry.

Q: Was Harry Smith sort of like the Alan Lomax of the urban setting?

AG: Yeah. He wound up in Boulder, at the Nairopa Institute, for the last couple years of his life. And the last year of his life he was brought back to New York to get a Grammy for his advancement of American folk music, along with Alan Lomax. So he recorded my sessions for *First Blues*, and the tapes were sitting around at Folkways Records, where Sam and Ann Charters found them, edited them, and put out the record. A great lineage. Both Harry Smith, who is a historically important figure in the blues, and Sam and Ann Charters, who are equally important. And then there was a later double album, by the same name, put out by the equally great John Hammond Sr. at Columbia Records. He recorded me in 1976, but Columbia wouldn't put it out because they thought it was too dirty.

Q: That album, I understand, has become quite a collector's item now.

AG: Yes. That record had the tune [singing] "Everybody's just a little bit homosexual / whether they like it or not ... Bomp bomp bomp." A little gay song. A lot of gay stuff on it, now that I think about it.

Q: Was that included on the boxed set that Rhino Records just put out of your material, *Holy Soul Jelly Roll?*

AG: Yes. Selections from it are on the Rhino CDs. One cut from the Harry Smith sessions, too. In fact, one of the cuts they didn't use. "Prayer Blues."

Q: You started recording music in the late 1960s with the William Blake songs that you had transcribed for music, right?

AG: Yes. Amazingly enough, though, I started writing songs, a very few songs, way back in the 1940s, and on that Rhino set there's a snippet of my voice singing one of those early gay Weltshmerz nostalgia songs from then. "The Green Valentine Blues." It's in my *Collected Poems*, and my new *Selected Poems*, and also the earliest thing on the Rhino CD set. It's a recording made on a home machine at John Clellon Holmes's house, in Old Saybrook, Connecticut, in 1949. Or maybe 1953. I forgot. But you are right, otherwise. I began recording my music, with the Blake songs, in 1969.

And then Bob Dylan heard me singing and improvising, and he came over and taught me a third chord. So I began improvising blues. Then I started recording with Dylan in 1971 and continued again in 1982. The Blake songs that were recorded in 1969 also had the help of jazz musicians Don Cherry and Elvin Jones. Charlie

Mingus advised me on musical styles. He was a neighbor. I sang at his wedding, actually. I was a specialist in mantra, coming from India, which is monochordal or modal music, and at that time Mingus and Coltrane and many others were sort of getting out of the complexity of bop and listening to the texture of sound with modal music, one chord variations. I was really good at that, so he invited me to sing at his wedding at Millbrook. So, anyway, I've been recording with musicians for quite some time.

Q: When I heard your new *The Ballad of the Skeletons*, it never struck me that it was anything but a natural progression for you.

AG: I'm not singing, really.

Q: But the musical backdrop seems perfectly natural, going back to those saxophone lines of poems like "Howl."

AG: I've done a lot of recording. I worked with Hal Wilner on something a couple of years ago called *The Lion for Real* that Mouth Almighty and Mercury Records, who is putting out *The Ballad of the Skeletons*, is going to reissue soon. They are also ready to have me complete the Blake project, do a complete set of the Blake songs. So I've got a couple of years of work already planned.

Q: Mercury Records seems to be doing some interesting things now. They recently put out a recording of Paul Krassner doing stand-up comedy, and next year they have a set of Timothy Leary recordings set to ambient music.

AG: I'm on the Tim Leary record, too. They recorded me reading some stuff I wrote about Leary, put a musical background on it.

Q: Specifically, about the songs on the new CD, "Ballad of the Skeletons" and "Amazing Grace," you are really effective at conveying your disgust with these various and sundry nogoodniks, but without lapsing into bitterness. This seems to be something that has always been a vital part of your poetry, too.

AG: Well, I started it at the time when the Contract with America was unveiled. Newt Gingrich and Rush Limbaugh seemed to be in the ascendancy and they seemed so full of ... well, s——.

Q: They are crawling out from under their rocks again.

AG: Yes, and it seems so hypocritical and so perverted. At the time I wrote "Ballad of the Skeletons," it seemed that someone had to take them on directly. The liberals in the nation seemed almost powerless in refuting them, when they were obviously such a bunch of double-crossers and hypocrites. Like the religious right. Where does the religious right get off condemning the poor when Christ says to take care of the poor? Where do they get off with this condemnation?

Q: It's always struck me that if a person could just stand back and not allow them to fill one with bitterness, they would eventually hang themselves on their own words.

AG: Well, you never can tell. Hitler didn't. They could bring on a disaster, like Netanyahu has in Israel. It's the step backwards that brings on the disasters. If they can save themselves now in the Middle East, it will be a miracle.

Q: The point I was trying to make with your "Ballad of the Skeletons" is that you do convey this sort of disgust, but there is an undercurrent of hope, and an edge of humor that has always been part of your poetry. . . . Gallows humor, for lack of a better term.

AG: There's also a recipe for the alternative. If you'll remember from the song, I sang, "Said the gnostic skeleton, the human form is divine. . . . Said the Buddhist skeleton, compassion is wealth. . . . Said the old Christ skeleton, care for the poor. . . . Said the Son of God skeleton, AIDS needs a cure. . . ." I'm giving the formula for the alternative, using very traditional, family-values sources. And I'm trying to point out the other things . . . "Said the ecological skeleton, keep skies blue . . ." I'm simply trying to point out the double-talk, hypocrisy, contradiction of the so-called right, in particular the monotheistic religious right, which is more like Stalinism.

Q: God as Stalin.

AG: He seems like such a pushover, frankly. They'll hoist him on their arches.

Q: Well, they pushed over Stalin's statues pretty damn quickly once the Cold War ended, so maybe that Stalin image is a nice image to have.

AG: Also I was inspired by the fact that, because of Jesse Helms, my poetry is banned from radio and television from 6 a.m. to 10 p.m. And so there was a part of that in the poem, the hypocrisy of how they talk about free and open markets, but they don't want to allow a free market of ideas. They dominate and monopolize the public communications.

Q: Unfortunately, I don't hold out much hope that Harvey Gantt can beat Helms.

AG: Really? … Another thing that should be noted about Jesse Helms … and I don't know if I've seen it elsewhere … has anybody examined Jesse Helms's emotional attitude toward gay life? Because it seems to me that no normal average heterosexual is as obsessed with homosexuality as he is.

Q: He does seem profoundly curious, way beyond the pale, so to speak.

AG: Obsessed. He is *always* on the subject.

Q: But it seems that the entire fundamentalist mindset is that way.

AG: At first, the *New York Times* used to say that this was just political demagoguery and don't pay any attention to it, it's not real. However, over the years, it seems to be Jesse's real psychological thing. In the S&M equation, he would be the top man. He wants to humiliate gays, and he has done that. But did you see that survey about homophobic students' reactions to gay pornography?

Q: No.

AG: When I was staying with Burroughs in July and August, it was reported in the local newspapers there, off the Reuters wire service. An experiment was done with college students. They took a group of heterosexual college students, some were homophobic and some were not. They showed them gay porn and attached some sort of wires to their bodies. The ones who were homophobic were aroused, the normal heterosexuals had no reaction at all.

Q: Where did they conduct this wild experiment? Certainly not Bob Jones University!

AG: Oh, some college. I have the clipping around here someplace. The thing that really has to be pointed out, published, whispered about, or trumpeted, is that Jesse Helms, Robert Dornan, and those people have some sort of thing about homosexuality. They have an obsession with it that no normal heterosexual has. An abnormal preoccupation. And it really is only a handful of Congressmen who are obsessed. The rest just sort of go along with it because they don't want to appear to be funny. But those guys are leading it, and yet their own sexuality is questionable. And it should be questioned. They don't need to be accused of being gay. It's just that their sexuality is already perverted in the sense that no normal heterosexual is interested in these matters as much as they are.

Q: Speaking of Congress, this leads me to a thought about where you fit in American letters. I've worked for the Library of Congress for years on publishing projects. Since it is the institution that houses the poet laureateship, I've wondered if they've ever contacted you about the possibility of being the U.S. poet laureate and, if not, why that is?

AG: I think Daniel Hoffman [poet laureate, 1973–1974] recommended me.

Q: And William Meredith [poet laureate, 1978–1980] did too, I've learned recently.

AG: Who makes the decision?

Q: I believe ultimately it is up to the Librarian of Congress, who is himself appointed by the president, more or less for life. James Billington is the current Librarian, and he was appointed by Ronald Reagan.

AG: Well, I haven't had a Pulitzer or a MacArthur [grant]. I don't need all that. I have more to do than I can possibly handle.

Q: And you probably wouldn't want to do it. But I can't think of anyone who has done more for American poetry and letters and been more generous with their time to other poets and writers. Joseph Brodsky, an exile from the Soviet Union, was named the poet laureate of the United States. It just seems like they could at least extend the courtesy to our own homegrown Brodsky. It would be kind of funny, though, wouldn't it? You'd have an office next door to the Supreme Court and across the street from the U.S. Capitol.

AG: I could really put on some interesting poetry readings. I'd get John Wieners to come down. Has he ever read at the Library?

Q: I don't think he has. But I know Gary Snyder has.

AG: I have. I read when Dan Hoffman was there. He invited me.

Q: Speaking of your generosity to younger poets, I wanted to thank you, belatedly, for a favor you did me years ago. I sent you a long poem that I'd written that I felt needed your guidance, and you wrote me back a very kind letter. You said the poem was a work of genius and should be translated into 26 languages. No, actually, you offered me some good advice and encouragement about the specific poem, and it was a very generous letter. It picked me up when I was down.

AG: If you still have the letter, please photocopy it and send it to me. Barry Miles [author of a 1989 Ginsberg biography and a 1993 biography of William Burroughs] is compiling my correspondence now. And I wrote a lot of letters, dashed them off, and never kept copies of them. Handwritten. God knows what I've said [laughs]. How old were you then?

Q: I don't know. In my early 30s. That was proof to me then that you are a worthy candidate for laureateship, that you carry on such exhaustive correspondence with no doubt hundreds, if not thousands, of aspiring young poets who seek you out. I read recently in the *Times*, in fact, that you now have a staff of three, just to handle paperwork.

AG: One person takes charge of the photographs I've done. One opens the mail and takes care of the mechanical sort of business. And one is a general secretary who takes care of management. And I answer what I can myself. It's just more than I could ever deal with.

Q: I'm sure it is. You're a touchstone to millions of people.

AG: Well, what it comes from is that William Carlos Williams answered me as a young poet, when I wrote him a note. He gave me very good advice, and he really turned me on to poetry, and gave me a direction in life. And I've always felt, well, it's up to me to pass that on.

Q: Well, you've done that and more, and I wish you continued health and vigor.

AG: I'm getting along. Keep an eye out for that MTV video of "Ballad of the Skeletons." Gus Van Zant did that, really a nice job. He did a video for Burroughs, and this one is almost as good.

Q: One final thing that I've always wanted to ask you about. You know, Michael Shumacher, who wrote one of your biographies [*Dharma Lion*, 1992], has just published a biography of Phil Ochs. I was wondering if you knew Ochs?

AG: Yes, quite well.

Q: He strikes me as so tragic but somehow culturally symbolic of the 1960s.

AG: I think it was alcohol and manic depression that killed him.

Q: But there is something that really lingers about him, besides his music. There's a real sense of his life as being a sort of rocket that inevitably had to return to earth, sort of like the 1960s themselves.

AG: Yes. Actually, I knew Phil so well that his brother asked me to wear his famous gold-lamé suit at a memorial concert for him at the Felt Forum. Nobody else would. They were afraid of it. But I'm a Buddhist. I'm not afraid of ghosts, so I put it on.

Q: My one book of poems, published years ago, was dedicated to Phil Ochs.

AG: He was a pioneer in political folk song.

Q: He was, and his later music was pointing in a new direction that was really quite moving, very touching, but so fragile. You could hear his personal fragility in his voice.

AG: One final thing about the musical matrix. For me, it was Shelley's "Mask of Anarchy" and Blake's "Let the Brothels of Paris Be Opened" about the French Revolution. There were traditions of certain kinds of political ballads and rhymes.

Ginsberg Redux: An Interview from 1996

Parke Puterbaugh also interviewed Allen Ginsberg in 1996. The following are some excerpts (reprinted with permission from Parke Puterbaugh) from that lengthy interview that are pertinent to a history of the Beatniks.

Ginsberg on the 1965 Albert Hall poetry reading: "We had quite large poetry readings here, maybe a thousand or two thousand in big halls, some very big readings at Harvard, Yale, Columbia. I was already used to masses of crowds listening to beatnik utterances. But there was something interesting about the Albert Hall: a lot of excitement, a lot of people, and nobody knew what to expect. There were a number of very good poets there, including Andre Voznesensky from Russia, as well as Gregory Corso and Lawrence Ferlinghetti. Indira Gandhi was up in the balcony! She sent me a note asking if we could get her better seats where she could see. So we got her downstairs sitting next to Voznesensky, who was forbidden to take part by his Russian handlers. I did him the homage of reading one of his poems, which was an attack on the Russian bureaucracy."

On the connections among black music, beat poetry, and rock 'n' roll: "The poets like Kerouac and myself and many others involved with what was called the Beat Generation literary movement were always interested in rhythm & blues and black music and bebop. Kerouac particularly, because Kerouac used to go up to Harlem and listen to Thelonious Monk, Lester Young, Roy Eldridge and everything like that. In the

Sixties, I spent months listening to Thelonius Monk at the Five Spot. We all grew up in the Fifties with Little Richard and *not* Elvis Presley. We listened to the actual black music—the Honeydrippers, Louis Jordan, Fats Domino. I had grown up with black spirituals in my neighborhood in Paterson, New Jersey. I listened to Leadbelly when I was a kid on WNYC in New York, where he had a half-hour weekly program. I'd always been very familiar with Ma Rainey, Bessie Smith, Billie Holiday, Bix Beiderbecke and all the old moldy-fig stuff, and so was Kerouac.

"So Kerouac was reflecting black street rhythms—well, let us say Bird and others were reflecting black street spoken rhythms, streetcorner rhythms. Kerouac was hearing those rhythms and turning them back into spoken language, poetry or prose. So there was already that alliance or recognition between black culture, black music, black rhythms and the new rhythms of the spoken language in American vernacular poetry.

"Then Bob Dylan. What Dylan told me when we were visiting Kerouac's grave in 1975 during the Rolling Thunder tour. . . . I pulled out a copy of Kerouac's *Mexico City Blues*, and Dylan grabbed the book and began reading from it. I said, 'What did you know about Kerouac's poetry?' He said, 'Oh, that was the first poetry I read. That woke me up to poetry.' I said, 'How come?' He said, 'Someone handed me a copy of it in St. Paul in 1958 or '59, and it blew my mind.' I said, 'Why?' And he said, 'It was the first poetry that spoke to me in my own language.'

"Dylan always saw Kerouac and myself as kind of inspirational and has said so many times. He came to New York to sing at the Gaslight Cafe, where we'd started coffeehouse poetry readings, which was also a new innovation—the idea of reading poetry in coffeehouses and bars. That would be around 1958 in New York and earlier, '56, in San Francisco. It evolved from San Francisco to New York when we went back home. The readings spread to other cafes and finally the St. Marks Poetry Project in the early Sixties."

On the Human Be-In in San Francisco: "A lot of people in San Francisco got together with the same idea, just like grunge kids get their own gangs together on Avenue A in New York today and have their own culture, their own community, their own friendships. Except we were doing it at a time when it was less well known to do that. There were precedents, like the Modernists of the Twenties—Ezra Pound, James Joyce and T. S. Eliot in Paris. The whole gang around Gertrude Stein, Hemingway, Fitzgerald and all that was a similar thing.

"So Haight-Ashbury was a continuation, another manifestation of things that had happened before in history. But it was like a coalescence of the free sexual revolution, the marijuana revolution, the drug revolution, political revolution, liberation movements of all kinds, getting together to have a Be-In. It was just to be there. That was the whole point. This was after the sit-ins, and the idea was more Buddhist influenced: to be there, to simply be there, not having to do anything particular except to enjoy the phenomena of being together outside of the realm of the state.

"It was just gangs of friends getting together. Gary Snyder and I circumambulated the meadow in Golden Gate Park, doing Hindu and Buddhist mantras to purify the ground. Suziki Roshi, the great Zen master, was seated on the platform in meditation most of the afternoon unbeknownst to most people, who didn't recognize him. The new bands, like Quicksilver and the Grateful Dead, were playing on the platform. It was a big poetry time, so Gary Snyder and Michael McClure and I read poems. Leary was allowed the same times as the poets, fifteen minutes. There was a psychedelic element there, too. We recruited the formerly hostile Hell's Angels to be the guardians. They weren't very good at it, but at least it neutralized them. Then at the end, we said, "Let's have kitchen yoga," which is to clean up the park as you leave. So we left the park cleaner than when we came, which was kind of astounding."

5. Jack Kerouac

The only people for me are the mad ones, the ones who are mad to live, mad to talk, mad to be saved, desirous of everything at the same time, the ones who never yawn or say a commonplace thing, but burn, burn, burn like fabulous yellow roman candles exploding like spiders across the stars and in the middle you see the blue centerlight pop and everybody goes "Awww!"
—narrator Sal Paradise, in *On the Road*

America, whither goest thou in thy shiny car in the night?
—attributed to Carlo Marx (character based on Allen Ginsberg), in *On the Road*

Woe, woe unto those who think that the Beat Generation means crime, delinquency, immorality, amorality ... woe unto those who attack it on the grounds that they simply don't understand history and the yearnings of human souls ... woe unto those who don't realize that America must, will, is, changing now, for the better I say ... woe unto those who make evil movies about the Beat Generation where innocent housewives are raped by beatniks! ... woe unto those who spit on the Beat Generation, the wind'll blow it back.

—from "Origins of the Beat Generation," *Playboy*, June 1959

I'd rather die than betray my faith in my work which is inseparable from my life, without this faith any kind of money is mockery ... there will be no American Literary Renaissance unless the sanctity of personal speech is honored, that indefinable personal quavering sound of each and every writer.

—from a March 4, 1957, letter to agent Sterling Lord, reacting to revisions of his work by the editors of *Evergreen Review*

6. Gary Snyder

Coyote the Nasty, the fat / Puppy that abused himself, the ugly gambler, / Bringer of goodies.

—from "A Berry Feast"

Lay down these words / Before your mind like rocks. / place solid, by hands.

—from "Riprap"

More Beat Words

Many other "Beats" have been cited over the years, though they are not among the originators of the movement. Among the ones most often affiliated with the Beat Generation or "Beatniks," are the following.

7. Ray Bremser

let me lay it to you gently, Mr. Gone! / fed up is what I'M!
—from "Poem of Holy Madness"

8. Lenny Bruce

Let me tell you the truth. The truth is what is. And what should be is a fantasy. A terrible terrible lie that someone gave the people long ago.

—from Bruce's regular stage routine

I'm not a comedian. I'm Lenny Bruce.

—from Bruce's regular stage routine, also found in *The Lenny Bruce Performance Film*

9. Lord Buckley

Hipsters, flipsters and finger-poppin' daddies, knock me your lobes. I came here to lay Caesar out, not to hop you to him. The bad jazz that a cat blows wails long after he's cut out. The groovy is often stashed with their frames. So don't put Caesar down.

—from the stage routine "Marc Antony's Funeral Oration," based on Shakespeare's *Julius Caesar*

10. Diane di Prima

The only war that matters is the war against the imagination. All others are subsumed in it.

—from "Rant"

11. Lawrence Ferlinghetti

I am waiting for my case to come up / and I am waiting / for a rebirth of wonder / and I am waiting for someone / to really discover America / and wail.

—from "I Am Waiting"

12. Ted Joans

Let's play something. Let's play anything. Let's play bohemian, and wear odd clothes, and grow a beard or a ponytail, live in the Village for 200.00 a month for one smallpad and stroll through Washington Square Park with a guitar and a chick looking sad.

—from "Let's Play Something"

I know a man who's neither white nor black / And his name is Jack Kerouac.
  —from *The Sermon*

13. LeRoi Jones (Amiri Baraka)

What can I say? / It is better to have loved and lost / Than to put linoleum in your living room?
  —from "In Memory of Radio"

14. Bob Kaufmann

On yardbird corners of embryonic hopes, drowned in a heroin tear.
  —from the poem "On"

15. Maynard G. Krebs

"Work?!"
  —signature quip, *The Many Loves of Dobie Gillis*

16. Tuli Kupferberg

Listen Square—You may kill the Beatnik but you will not kill the Beatnik in yourself.
  —from *The War Against the Beats*

129. Walk into the induction center carrying an octopus.
  —from "1001 Ways to Beat the Draft"

17. Philip Lamantia

I am worn like an old sack by a celestial bum / I'm dropping my eyes where all the trees turn on fire! / I'm mad to go to you, Solitude— who will carry me there?
  —from "High"

18. Michael McClure

I AM MOVING IN THE YELLOW KITCHEN / high never to come down—the ceiling brown. / I am looking at the face of the red clock—meaningless.
  —from "Peyote Poem"

Interview

Michael McClure was one of the poets who read at the Six Gallery on the occasion of Allen Ginsberg's public unveiling of his monumental poem "Howl." That reading, which took place on October 13, 1955, is one of the red-letter dates in Beatnik history. McClure, a young poet, migrated to San Francisco in 1954 to study art at San Francisco State College, where he met Ruth Witt-Diamant, who ran the Poetry Center. There, McClure took a poetry workshop with Robert Duncan, which turned his attentions to the written word. Soon thereafter, he took part in the landmark 1955 poetry reading at the Six Gallery in San Francisco. Over the years, McClure was a central figure in the transference of the Beatnik mystique to the burgeoning hippie movement. He would go on to befriend and work with Jim Morrison of the Doors (and, in the 1990s, with Ray Manzarek of the Doors) He wrote the controversial play *The Beard* (1966), as well as collaborated with Hell's Angel leader Frank Reynolds on the latter's memoir, *Freewheelin' Frank: Secretary of the Angels* (1967).

Parke Puterbaugh, a long-time *Rolling Stone* editor and contributor and consultant to the Rock and Roll Hall of Fame in Cleveland, interviewed McClure in 1998 about the confluence of countercultures in the Bay Area that McClure had help foster. The following are some excerpts from the interview (reprinted with Puterbaugh's permission).

PP: Why do you think that San Francisco was the staging area for so many scenes segueing one into the other?
MM: It goes back to anarchist workingmen's circles. Originally in the early 1950s, San Francisco was like a cross between a harbor town and cow town. The tallest building in the city was 12 or 15 stories, and there was this beautiful waterfront that looked onto Asia. It didn't look to New York. Maybe it looked to London more than to anywhere in America. Maybe a bit to Paris too. But it wasn't really a part of the United States. There was a different set of rules. You would walk down the street hearing people talking Chinese or Japanese, which was really interesting at the time. You would run into people who were honest to god Buddhists, they didn't just go around saying they were. They practiced Buddhism. And Chinese

philosophy, like the ancient ones, was studied by a lot of people, including working men as well as poets. From here you could go to the mountains, you could go to Mt. Tamalpais [across the Golden Gate Bridge in Marin County] in those days in your old car with the door tied shut with rope cause somebody gave it to you and the door wasn't fixed. You could drive from your place in the Haight to the top of Mt. Tamalpais at whatever speed your car would go, because there wasn't any traffic.... You could drive up to a redwood forest, Muir Woods. If you could get someone with a slightly better car than yours you could all get together and drive to Death Valley and look at the wildflowers in the spring. You get somebody with a car that good you could drive to Big Sur and go down and see what's now called Esalen Hot Springs. What's the Esalen Institute, it was Slade's Hot Springs, and it was a bunch of funny old bathtubs hanging on a wooden platform on the side of the cliff and hot water came out. And Henry Miller would be there and artist Ephraim Doner. That's one of the places we went one night. Kerouac talking about that in *Big Sur*.

So you have this opening to Asia, both philosophically and conceptually, and you are on the Pacific Rim, and you can literally touch forest, ocean, river, bay, mountain, and it's easy and it's beautiful.... So you have that, and then you have I think because of the anarchist workingmen's circles, a very liberal reputation for San Francisco. As there was for Seattle, too, except it needed a better climate, needed to be more dry. I grew up in Seattle. I could see it had to be drier. And so during World War II when there was that Conscientious Objectors camp in Waldport, Oregon, these COs started coming down here on their paroles or when they got out. You had poets like William Everson and poet-workingmen like James Harmon coming down here. You had a crew of people coming down here from the CO camps and the literary bunch of them ties up with Kenneth Rexroth, who's an old anarchist philosopher poet of extreme brilliance. As a matter of fact, he was instrumental in helping a lot of young people see what was going on, I mean where we were in terms of like he did a lot of hiking, knew nature and knew a lot about Asian philosophy and Asian art. They would hook up with him and he had an open house, so then you get and there were other literary movements here, too ...

PP: What period would that have been?

MM: The early and middle 1950s. Then there was the super bo-hemian group. I think the first poetry reading I went to here had belly dancing and bongo drums. It wasn't anybody that was on par with the Beats but it was pretty far out. So the Bay Area has that kind of richness, and then Rexroth once said, it also had North Beach. He said about San Francisco that it was to the world as Bar-celona was to the Spanish anarchists.... We had connections to other traditions, too. Philip Lamantia, a young poet, who was accepted by Andre Breton [French writer who drew up the "mani-festo" for the Surrealist movement] as one of the great living surreal-ist poets, this kid. And he was one of the first people I met in the city. He was in the first reading, at the Six Gallery, with us.

PP: In particular you and Ginsberg seemed to link up with some of the newer things that began happening in the wake of the San Francisco Poetry Renaissance, particularly the Human Be-In type things but also the musical groups. There seemed to be a permeable border there.

MM: It was more than permeable; it was permeated. It was all interpenetrated. A friend of mine once said everyone was an artist who did something really well, whether they were a saddle maker or played the bass. I thought that was an interesting comment. I met Allen Ginsberg early in 1955 at a party for W. H. Auden after Auden's reading at the Poetry Center [at San Francisco State Col-lege], at the home of Ruth Witt-Diamant [director of the Poetry Center]. Allen and I were both like the wallflowers at this party, because we were the youngest people in a room full of mostly pro-fessors. Actually, Allen knew Auden slightly and he talked to him a bit, but Allen and I were more interested in each other. We talked about William Blake, our ideas about Blake, and we began together after that and he showed me Kerouac's work. I was very taken with *Mexico City Blues*, and still am. I think it's one of the great religious poems in the contemporary world, at least in English.

PP: You talked about everyone was doing all sorts of things at once, and I'm trying to draw this linear thing from poets of the late 1950s, early 1960s segueing into musicians from the mid to late 1960s. It's not really that neat or tidy, is it?

MM: Think of it a different way. It isn't a segue. It is an interpen-tration. It's not happening just on one front. This is like people who have known each other for a long time coming together in different ways, people coming in from out of town, people leaving, people going away, a huge fluid scene developing with a philosophy and an attractive, strange newspaper to go with it and a new art form that's very catchy, rock. And some of it's not really rock. Some is more interesting than rock.

PP: I always liked some of the raga-like qualities of the rock jamming that would go on at the Bay Area concerts.

MM: You might have liked our band Freewheelin' McClure Montana. We were really loopy. We sounded like a cross between country music and raga. It's a simultaneously permeability of people overlapping each other for what had been a number of second existences: jug band scenes or poet groups or painter cliques. And you gotta remember there weren't very many artists around in those days. When we first went up to the Six Gallery, I'm talking like there was a big literary scene. It's not that there was a big literary scene, there was a very tiny literary scene. You knew every poet in the Bay Area because it took some nerve to say you were a poet. They would yell fairy at you and try hanging you from a lamppost. A lot of people who were artists went to North Beach and used it like a reservation where they weren't going to get tromped or beat up.

PP: Beat up by longshoremen?

MM: No, the longshoremen were OK. Longshoremen were fine. Most of us worked one time or another in all those unions. Longshoremen were liable to be pretty far out. No, it was the general mood of America at the time: sneering, bitter conformity and great inner stress and lack of diversity and finding some way to carry that fucking war on to pay for things, dragging it into Asia. Made people really ugly. Gotta remember what we were doing wasn't the Fifties. It was an alternative to the Fifties. The Fifties were ugly. I'm not talking about the good old days. Things are pretty sweet, even if the corporations seem to be winning the war.... But there's a higher percentage of people who have some idea of what's going on. And *Rolling Stone* had some part in that. I remember Michael Lydon brought me the first copy of *Rolling Stone*. He swung by my place and laid a copy on me. I said, "A magazine about rock 'n' roll?" He said, "Yeah, and I'm quitting my job at *Newsweek*." I told him, "You don't know what you're doing!" I mean there just weren't a lot of people around interested in this. But by the Sixties there was a big scene of young people coming out of the bushes and out of America.

PP: I've read Jack Kerouac most of my life and I've always been curious as to why he did not get closer to rock 'n' roll.

MM: Jack was very very close to jazz, as you know. It was probably easier for me because Jack was ten years older than me. Allen was 7 or 8 years older than me, although Allen didn't have any trouble. There is a little age factor between some of the East Coast Beats are an older bunch, in general. There's two or three of them, and they're pretty much a different generation and it was pretty much coming out here that really turned the thing over and brought it to life and it quit being urban guys hugging each other, kissing each other, jumping into bed and driving cars around, and it got kind of real. When Kerouac heard Gary Snyder reading and me reading and other people reading at the Six Gallery, then he wanted to go out into the forest and do fire-watching. Kerouac got turned on to the nature. The urban kid got turned on to nature by West Coast Beats, who are the San Francisco Renaissance, call it whatever you want, who were it always seemed to me the literary wing of the environmental movement in the beginning when there was no other literary wing to the environmental movement. That's what we were talking about. Not just the politics of the U.S. or the sociology or the psychology but also what's going on in the forests and ocean and air and water and overcrowding. When we went to places like Paris, we actually got booed in Paris for talking about this, they said "elitists" to us! They thought we were ignoramuses. And now I have some friends who were at those things who say, "You guys were right back then, how did you know that stuff?" Maybe you had to be in San Francisco to know it.

PP: What is your view of Ginsberg's role in this whole thing in terms of furthering what was going on?

MM: Well, "Howl" was certainly critical to what was going on. I think the whole Six Gallery reading was critical because there is still a tendency to look at the Beat Generation thing as William Burroughs, Allen Ginsberg and Jack Kerouac, and that may be how it looks from New York. But that really ignores the fact of what a turn on San Francisco was for Kerouac and Allen.

19. Norman Mailer

In such places as Greenwich Village, a ménage-a-trois was completed—the bohemian and the juvenile delinquent came face-to-face with the Negro, and the hipster was a fact in American life.
—from the essay "The White Negro"

20. Jack Micheline

There is nothing deeper than life and the livers of life / mankind raped in the bank vaults of steel / dead soldiers, battlefields surrounded by iron and ironies.
—from "Poet of the Streets"

21. Kenneth Patchen

Do the dead know what time it is?
—from *Because It Is*

The argument of innocence can only be lost if it is won.
—from *Painted Poems*

All at once is what eternity is.
—from *Painted Poems*

22. Kenneth Rexroth

You killed him! You killed him. / In your God damned Brooks Brothers Suit, / You son of a bitch.
—from "Thou Shalt Not Kill," an ode on the death of Dylan Thomas

23. Mort Sahl

Liberals feel unworthy of their possessions. Conservatives feel they deserve everything they've stolen.
—from *Heartland*

24. Jack Spicer

The birds are still in flight. Believe the birds.
    —from "Imaginary Elegies"

25. Lew Welch

You can't fix it. You can't make it go away. / I don't know what you're going to do about it, / But I know what I'm going to do about it. I'm just going to walk away from it. Maybe / A small part of it will die if I'm not around / feeding it anymore.
    —from "Chicago Poem"

When I drive cab / I end the only lit and waitful thing in miles of darkened houses.
    —from "Taxi Suite"

26. Vachel Lindsay

Keep away from cities; Have nothing to do with money; Ask for dinner about quarter after eleven.
    —from *A Handy Guide for Beggars*

Selected Bibliography

Publications

Allen, Donald, ed. *The New American Poetry*. New York: Grove Press, 1960.

Amram, David. *Collaborating with Kerouac*. New York: Thunder's Mouth Press, 2002.

Anderson, Elliott, and Mary Kinzie, eds. *The Little Magazine in America: A Modern Documentary History*. Yonkers, NY: Pushcart Press, 1978.

Beard, Rick, and Leslie Cohen Berlowitz, eds. *Greenwich Village: Culture and Counterculture*. New Brunswick, NJ: Rutgers University Press, 1993.

Bisbort, Alan. "Hats Off to Harper." www.gadflyonline.com, 2000.

———. "Keeper of Kerouac's Flame." *Hartford Advocate*, April 27, 1995, 21.

———. *Media Scandals*. Westport, CT: Greenwood Press, 2008.

Brinkley, Douglas. "The Kerouac Papers." *Atlantic Monthly*, November 1998, 50–75.

Bruce, Lenny. *How to Talk Dirty and Influence People*. New York: Fireside, 1992.

Campbell, James. *This Is the Beat Generation*. London: Secker and Warburg, 1999.

Cassady, Carolyn. *Off the Road: My Years with Cassady, Kerouac and Ginsberg*. New York: Penguin Books, 1991.

Cassady, Neal, and Allen Ginsberg. *As Ever: The Collected Correspondence of Allen Ginsberg and Neal Cassady*. Berkeley, CA: Creative Arts, 1977.

Charters, Ann. *Kerouac: A Biography*. New York: Warner Books, 1974.

Charters, Ann, ed. *The Portable Beat Reader*. New York: Viking, 1992.

Christopher, Tom. "Neal Cassady: Volume One, 1926–1940." Self-published, 1995.

Clarke, Gerald. *Capote*. Cambridge, MA: Da Capo, 2005.

Cook, Bruce. *The Beat Generation*. New York: Charles Scribner's Sons, 1971.

Dawson, Fielding. *The Black Mountain Book*. New York: Croton Press, 1970.

Douglas, Ann. "City Where the Beats Were Moved to Howl." *New York Times*, December 26, 1997, B41, B47.

Ferlinghetti, Lawrence, and Nancy J. Peters. *Literary San Francisco*. San Francisco: City Lights Books/Harper and Row, 1980.

Fisher, Stanley. *Beat Coast East: An Anthology of Rebellion*. New York: Excelsior, 1960.

Frank, Robert. *The Americans*. New York: Pantheon, 1986.

George-Warren, Holly, ed. *The Rolling Stone Book of the Beats: The Beat Generation and American Culture*. New York: Hyperion, 1999.

A "gonzo" anthology written and compiled by participants and those of the 1960s generation who were influenced by the Beats. Among contributors are David Amram, Lester Bangs, David Bowie, Johnny Depp, Michael McClure, Graham Parker, Patti Smith, Hunter S. Thompson, photographers Robert Frank and Mellon, Parke Puterbaugh (who contributed to this book), and Richard Meltzer, whose "Another Superficial Piece about 158 Beatnik Books" is an indispensable if eccentric overview of the best and worst of the Beat Generation writings.

Gewirtz, Isaac. *Beatific Soul: Jack Kerouac on the Road*. London: Scala, 2007.

Published in conjunction with an exhibition at the New York Public Library commemorating the 50th anniversary of the publication of *On the Road*. The book contains never-before-published sketches, paintings, and facsimiles of journal and manuscript pages by Kerouac. It also offers deep insights into Kerouac's creative processes and his own dictums on that score (e.g., "Stop When You Want to 'Improve.' It's Done"). The author is the curator of the library's Berg Collection, which contains the Jack Kerouac Archive.

Gifford, Barry, and Lawrence Lee. *Jack's Book: An Oral Biography of Jack Kerouac*. New York: St. Martin's, 1978.

Ginsberg, Allen. *Allen Verbatim: Lectures on Poetry, Politics, Consciousness*. Edited by Gordon Ball. New York: McGraw-Hill, 1974.

———. *The Book of Martyrdom and Artifice: First Journals and Poems, 1937–1952*. Cambridge, MA: Da Capo, 2006.

———. "The Hipster's Hipster." *New York Times Magazine*, December 29, 1996, 39. Obituary and recollection of Herbert Huncke.

———. *Journals Mid-Fifties, 1954–1958*. Edited by Gordon Ball. New York: HarperCollins, 1995.

———. *The Letters of Allen Ginsberg*. Edited by Bill Morgan. Cambridge, MA: Da Capo, 2008.

Goodyear, Dana. "Zen Master." *The New Yorker*, October 20, 2008, 66–75. Profile of Gary Snyder.

Holmes, John Clellon. *Go*. New York: Thunder's Mouth, 1997.

———. "The Philosophy of the Beat Generation." *Esquire*, February 1958, 35–38.

Johnson, Joyce. *Minor Characters*. Boston: Houghton Mifflin, 1983.

Jones, Hettie. *How I Became Hettie Jones*. New York: Grove Press, 1996.

Kaufman, Michael T. "At 78, Someone Who Is Still Beat yet Undefeated." *New York Times*, December 9, 1992, B3.

Kerouac, Jack. "Aftermath: The Philosophy of the Beat Generation." *Esquire*, March 1958, 24–26.

Kerouac, Jack. *Selected Letters, 1940–1956*. Edited by Ann Charters. New York: Viking, 1995.

——. *Selected Letters, 1957–1969*. Edited by Ann Charters. New York: Viking, 1999.

Kilgannon, Corey. "A Distinguished Professor with a Ph.D. in Nonsense." *New York Times*, April 14, 2008.

Knight, Arthur, and Kit Knight, eds. *Beat Angels*. California, PA: Self-published, 1982.

Knight, Brenda. *Women of the Beat Generation*. Berkeley, CA: Conari Press, 1996.

Krim, Seymour. *What's This Cat's Story?: The Best of Seymour Krim*. New York: Paragon House, 1991.

Krim, Seymour, ed. *The Beats*. Greenwich, CT: Gold Medal Books, 1963.

Lipton, Lawrence. *The Holy Barbarians*. New York: Julian Messner, Inc., 1959.

McDarrah, Fred W., and Timothy McDarrah. *Kerouac and Friends: A Beat Generation Album*. New York: Thunder's Mouth, 2002.
  An essential book of photographic evidence, as well as detailed biographies and contributions from many neglected participants in the Beat Generation.

McNally, Dennis. *Desolate Angel: Jack Kerouac, the Beat Generation, and America*. New York: Random House, 1979.

Miles, Barry. *The Beat Hotel: Ginsberg, Burroughs, and Corso in Paris, 1957–1963*. New York: Grove Press, 2000.

——. *Ginsberg: A Biography*. New York: Simon and Schuster, 1989.

——. *William Burroughs: El Hombre Invisible*. New York: Hyperion, 1993.

Nicosia, Gerald. *Memory Babe: A Critical Biography of Jack Kerouac*. New York: Grove Press, 1983.

O'Neil, Paul. "The Only Rebellion Around: But the Shabby Beats Bungle the Job in Arguing, Sulking and Bad Poetry. *Life*, November 30, 1959, 114–130.

Plummer, William. *The Holy Goof: A Biography of Neal Cassady*. Englewood Cliffs, NJ: Prentice-Hall, 1981.

Rivers, Larry, with Arnold Weinstein. *What Did I Do?: The Unauthorized Autobiography*. New York: HarperCollins, 1992.

Sahl, Mort. *Heartland*. New York: Harcourt Brace Jovanovich, 1976.

Saroyan, Aram. *Genesis Angels: The Saga of Lew Welch and the Beat Generation*. New York: William Morrow, 1979.

Schleifer, Marc. "The Beat Debated." *Village Voice*, November 19, 1958.

Silesky, Barry. *Ferlinghetti: The Artist in His Time*. New York: Warner Books, 1990.

Spengler, Oswald. *The Decline of the West*. New York: Knopf, 1962.

Spicer, Jack. *My Vocabulary Did This to Me: The Collected Poetry of Jack Spicer.* Middletown, CT: Wesleyan University Press, 2008.

Stone, Robert. *Prime Green.* New York: Ecco, 2007.

Sukenick, Ronald. *Down and In: Life in the Underground.* New York: Collier, 1987.

Thompson, Toby. "The Happy Buddha of Kitkitdizze." *Outside*, November 1993, 58–64, 162–167.

Profile of Gary Snyder.

Tytell, John. *Paradise Outlaws: Remembering the Beats.* Photographs by Mellon. New York: William Morrow, 1999.

Watson, Steven. *The Birth of the Beat Generation: Visionaries, Rebels, and Hipsters, 1944–1960.* New York: Pantheon, 1995.

A detailed and entertaining history of the hundreds of threads that made up the Beat Generation tapestry.

Wolcott, James. "Kerouac's Lonesome Road." *Vanity Fair*, October 1999, 126–137.

Essential Reading

William S. Burroughs

Junky (1953). A straightforward account of Burroughs's drug addiction, and his unorthodox methods of kicking the habit.

Naked Lunch (1959). When this novel was published in 1959, Terry Southern called it "An absolutely devastating ridicule of all that is false, primitive, and vicious in current American life."

Neal Cassady

As Ever: The Collected Correspondence of Allen Ginsberg and Neal Cassady (1977). Contains Cassady's best available writing, including some wild and hilarious tales from the road.

The First Third (1971). An attempt at a "serious" memoir of his life that he left unfinished (the memoir and his life, one might say). The best parts are the letters to Kerouac and friends, and transcripts of his conversations. The reader can see how the "flow" of Cassady's mind influenced these other Beat writers, from this evidence.

Gregory Corso

Elegiac Feelings American (1970). A book-length tribute to Jack Kerouac, written in homage to his friend after his death in 1969.

The Happy Birthday of Death (1960). Contains Corso's most-often anthologized work, including "Marriage," "Bomb," "Food," and "Death."

Lawrence Ferlinghetti

A Coney Island of the Mind (1958). One of the best-selling books of modern poetry; contains his long jazz-poem "I Am Waiting."

Allen Ginsberg

Howl and Other Poems
Kaddish and Other Poems, 1958–1960
Selected Poems, 1947–1995
Journals: Early Fifties Early Sixties (edited by Gordon Ball)
Allen Verbatim: Lectures on Poetry, Politics, Consciousness by Allen Ginsberg (edited
    by Gordon Ball)
Journals Mid-Fifties, 1954–1958 (edited by Gordon Ball)
The Letters of Allen Ginsberg (edited by Bill Morgan)

LeRoi Jones

Dutchman and *The Slave* (1964). Two controversial, award-winning plays pub-
    lished together.
Preface to a Twenty Volume Suicide Note (1961). These early poems were written
    during a time when Jones was involved with the Beats.

Jack Kerouac

On the Road. Several editions of this classic exist: (1) the Viking Critical Library
    edition, which includes the text of the book, critical essays, and the transcript
    of Kerouac's *Paris Review* "Writers at Work" interview; (2) the Original
    Scroll edition, the April 1951 version that Kerouac typed in three weeks on a
    120-foot sheet of paper (Viking); (3) facsimile hardcover edition of the 1957
    hardcover first edition (Viking); and (4) the standard trade paperback of the
    1957 version (Signet). Other essential Kerouac novels are *Big Sur*, *The
    Dharma Bums*, *Maggie Cassidy*, *The Subterraneans*, *Vanity of Duluoz*, and
    Visions of Cody. Also worth reading is *Lonesome Traveler*, a collection of prose
    pieces, mostly nonfiction work.
Jack Kerouac Road Novels, 1957–1960 (edited by Douglas Brinkley): The Library
    of America has produced a sturdy one-volume edition of Kerouac's early
    works. Included in their entirety are the novels *On the Road*, *The Dharma
    Bums*, *The Subterraneans*, and *Tristessa*, as well as *Lonesome Traveler* (a collec-
    tion of travel writings) and some journal selections.
The Portable Jack Kerouac (edited by Ann Charters) contains excerpts from all the
    major novels of "The Legend of Duluoz," excerpts from his books of poems;
    his most important essays on "spontaneous prose"; excerpts from the esoteric
    books *Visions of Cody*, *Book of Dreams*, and *Old Angel Midnight*; essays on
    "bop and the Beat Generation"; writings on Buddhism; selected letters; and
    an "identity key" to the named characters in Kerouac's fiction.
Selected Letters, two volumes: *1940–1956* and *1957–1969* (edited by Ann Char-
    ters). Because Kerouac's fiction so closely mirrored his own life and experien-
    ces, his letters form the nucleus of his published novels. At times, the letters
    outpace the novels for the sheer enormity of their vision, scope, and passion
    as well as the peerless writing talent.

Windblown World: The Journals of Jack Kerouac, 1947–1954 (edited by Douglas Brinkley): A collection of Kerouac's journals, in which he mapped out many of the themes he would pursue in his books. No better document exists as a testament to the shaping of a young American writer.

Michael McClure

The Beard (1965). This play caused a sensation when it was performed, leading to obscenity charges and packed houses on both coasts.

Scratching the Beat Surface (1982). These selected essays, interviews, and poems are the best starting point for an introduction to McClure's work.

Gary Snyder

Turtle Island (1975), and *Mountains and Rivers Without End* (1996).

Films

The Beat Generation: An American Dream (1987). Directed by Janet Forman. Contains interviews with most of the major literary figures of the Beat Generation, but few others beside writers. Jack Kerouac and Neal Cassady are represented by archival footage.

Drugstore Cowboy (1989). Written and directed by Gus Van Sant, based on a true-life novel by James Fogle. This feature film starred Matt Dillon and Kelly Lynch and featured an appearance by William S. Burroughs as a defrocked priest who offers sage advice to the young addicts about the dangers of temptation. The film was critically acclaimed, as was Burroughs in his small part.

Go Moan for Man: The Literary Odyssey of Jack Kerouac (1998). Written and directed by Doug Sharples. A docudrama with scenes of Beatnik glory depicted by Bill Mabon (as Jack Kerouac). Commentary provided by Ann Charters, Dennis McNally, Gerald Nicosia, and John Tytell. Many of Kerouac's friends and companions were interviewed for the film, including his wives Stella Sampas and Edie Parker, his daughter Jan Kerouac, David Amram, William S. Burroughs, Gregory Corso, Lawrence Ferlinghetti, Allem Ginsberg, John Clellon Holmes, Joyce Johnson, Ken Kesey, agent Sterling Lord, and Michael McClure.

The Lenny Bruce Performance Film (2005). Filmed at the Basin Street West in San Francisco in 1965, the second-to-last live performance before his death. DVD also includes the brilliant, legendary animated short film, "Thank You Mask Man," the story for which Bruce wrote and narrated (now a popular item on YouTube).

The Life and Times of Allen Ginsberg (2006). Written and directed by Jerry Aronson. An exceptionally detailed documentary that includes rare footage of Ginsberg and Cassady in conversation at City Lights Books in San Francisco and Ginsberg standing with Bob Dylan at Jack Kerouac's grave.

Pull My Daisy (1959). Written and narrated by Jack Kerouac. Directed by
Alfred Leslie, cinematography by Robert Frank, music by David Amram.
A free viewing of this quintessential Beatnik movie can be found on
Google film.

The Source: A Film of the Beat Generation (1999). Written and directed by Chuck
Workman. Half documentary/half dramatization, the footage includes rare
and offbeat interviews, home movies, TV appearances, and reminiscences by
and about the major players of the Beat pantheon. Excerpts from Beat literature are read by Johnny Depp, Dennis Hopper, and John Turturro. The film
flashes back, as well as forward, commenting on the impacts the Beatniks
had on the counterculture of the 1960s and 1970s.

Village Sunday (1963). A short but evocative report on life in Greenwich Village,
narrated by Jean Shepard, who insists, "In the Village everybody's young
inside." The film, which is available on YouTube, has an excellent jazzy
soundtrack and closes with Beat poet Ted Joans reading from "The Sermon"
(e.g., "You must love your life out").

What Happened to Kerouac? (1986). Cowritten and directed by Lewis MacAdams
and Richard Lerner. An excellent documentary featuring the faces and voices
of major Beat figures like William S. Burroughs, Neal and Carolyn Cassady,
Gregory Corso, Lawrence Ferlinghetti, Allen Ginsberg, Michael McClure,
and Gary Snyder, as well as Steve Allen and William F. Buckley Jr. The
soundtrack is a nearly seamless melding of the music of one of Kerouac's
favorite jazz artist, Thelonious Monk.

Recordings

The Beat Generation (Rhino, 1992). An indispensable box-set collection of writers
and performers who defined, or were defined by, the Beatnik era: Writers
include Allen Ginsberg, Jack Kerouac, Kenneth Patchen, and Kenneth
Rexroth. Performers include Lenny Bruce, Lord Buckley, Slim Gaillard, and
Babs Gonzalez; musicians include David Amram, Dexter Gordon, Gerry
Mulligan, and Charlie Parker.

The Jack Kerouac Collection (Rhino, 1990). This three-CD box set contains essential recordings of Kerouac reading to Steve Allen's piano accompaniment;
and to Zoot Sims's and Al Cohn's saxophone improvisations.

Jack Kerouac Reads On the Road (Rykodisc, 1999). David Amram's musical
arrangements bring some order to a collection that includes Kerouac singing
"Ain't We Got Fun" and "Come Rain or Come Shine," and reading excerpts
from his work, including rarities like "Washington D.C. Blues" (written at
poet laureate Randall Jarrell's house).

Kerouac Kicks Joy Darkness (Rykodisc, 1997). An assortment of artists influenced
by the Beats read or perform or interpret excerpts from Jack Kerouac's writings. These include Eric Andersen, William S. Burroughs, John Cale (of the
Velvet Underground), Jim Carroll, Johnny Depp, Matt Dillon, Allen

Ginsberg, Juliana Hatfield, Patti Smith, Sonic Youth, Joe Strummer, Hunter S. Thompson, and Warren Zevon.

Beat Collections

Bancroft Library, University of California, Berkeley.

This venerable institution holds the Lawrence Ferlinghetti Papers, which are comprised of "literary manuscripts: Notes, poetry fragments, single poems, poetry collections, plays, and prose works of fiction and non-fiction, largely holograph mss. and typescripts with holograph revisions; travel journals dating from 1960–1986; notebooks; musical compositions by various composers based on poems of Ferlinghetti." There is a separate collection for the City Lights Books Records.

Bancroft Library also has the largest holdings of several others affiliated with the Beats. These include the papers for Richard Brautigan, Ted Joans, Philip Lamantia, Michael McClure, Jack Micheline, Jack Spicer, and Philip Whalen.

Department of Special Collections, General Library, University of California, Davis.

The Gary Snyder Papers "document the personal and professional activities of Gary Snyder (b. 1930), poet, essayist, translator, Zen Buddhist, environmentalist, lecturer, and teacher. Snyder is considered one of the most significant environmental writers of the twentieth century and a central figure in environmental activism. He wrote more than twenty books of poetry and prose including his forty-year work *Mountains and Rivers Without End* and *Turtle Island* for which he won the 1975 Pulitzer Prize for Poetry. The collection spans the years 1910–2003 (1945–2002 bulk) and continues to grow. Drafts as well as final versions of poems and prose pieces are found in the collection along with correspondence, recordings of poetry readings and interviews, subject files, manuscripts and publications by other authors, serials, ephemera, and memorabilia."

Department of Special Collections, University of California, Santa Cruz.

The Kenneth Patchen Archive contains "original manuscripts, extensive set of outgoing and incoming correspondence, first and subsequent editions of his books, limited painted book editions, original Painted Poems, scrapbooks, recordings, paintings and other art work. Bulk of the material dates between 1929–1972."

Department of Special Collections and Archives, Kent Main Campus Library, Kent State University

This archive contains the John Clellon Holmes Papers and Recordings, as well as some letters of Gary Snyder.

Green Library, Department of Special Collections, Stanford University, Palo Alto, California. The Allen Ginsberg Papers collection "contains approximately 300,000 items, everything from journals, tapes, letters, poems in progress, newspaper and beard clippings, even dried-up pieces of hallucinogenic vines and a pair of old tennis shoes."

Green Library also has two special collections that contain original manuscripts, correspondence, and other archival materials related to Gregory Corso.

The Henry W. and Albert A. Berg Collection of English and American Literature, New York Public Library, New York City.

The collection contains the Jack Kerouac Archive, as well as the archives of William S. Burroughs and Terry Southern, who is sometimes associated with the Beat Generation.

Mandeville Special Collections Library, University of California, San Diego.

Lew Welch Papers; Donald Allen Papers; Some Gary Snyder letters.

The Thomas J. Dodd Center, University of Connecticut, Storrs, Connecticut.

This facility, attached to the university library, contains the archives of Beat scholar, poet, and publisher Ed Sanders, as well as those of Abbie Hoffman, who was deeply influenced by the Beats and often appeared at latter-day conferences devoted to the Beat Generation. The Archives and Special Collections at the Dodd Center also contain a small cache of Lawrence Ferlinghetti material, the Ed Dorn Papers, the Joel Oppenheimer Papers, and the Diane Di Prima Papers, which contain correspondence, books, personal papers, manuscripts, publications, photographs, audiotapes, fliers (printed matter). Also included are journals and diaries, poetry and a manuscript of *Memoirs of a Beatnik*.

The Dodd Center also holds the papers of Ann Charters, who taught English at the university for many years. Charters's archive contains letters and photographs related to the Beats. Finally, the Dodd Center holds the Charles Olson Research Collection, the largest assemblage of material by this major figure in American literature who taught at Black Mountain College and influenced many writers in the Beat circle.

Worthy Web Sites

Beat Scene. http://www.beatscene.net/index.asp.

A magazine that bills itself as "the voice of the Beat Generation." Though it is based in England, much of the unique and always entertaining content is available at its Web site.

Literary Kicks. http://www.litkicks.com/beatgen.

Founded in 1994 by Levi Asher while "pretending to work on PowerPoint presentations at the Wall Street headquarters of JP Morgan." The site's stated mission is to "explore the meaning and relevance of literature in modern life." When it was created, LitKicks was dedicated solely to the Beat Generation. Its "Beat News" is considered one of the earliest literary blogs on the Internet. LitKicks has since sponsored poetry contests and writing tournaments, held 24-hour poetry parties, published books, and expanded its mission into college classrooms.

Index

About the Author

ALAN BISBORT has been collecting material on the Beat Generation for the past three decades. During the 17 years he worked on staff at the Library of Congress (1977–1994), he utilized the General Collections and custodial divisions while researching the subject and amassed files of photocopies of some rare and unusual material. *Beatniks*, which shares much of that research material, is written for readers to use as both a reference tool and an engaging, informed overview of this complex but fascinating subject. Bisbort has written extensively about American culture and the arts as a columnist, reporter, blogger, and author of several other books, as well as contributor to *Rolling Stone*, *Creem*, the *New York Times*, and the *Washington Post*. His previous book for Greenwood Press was *Media Scandals*.

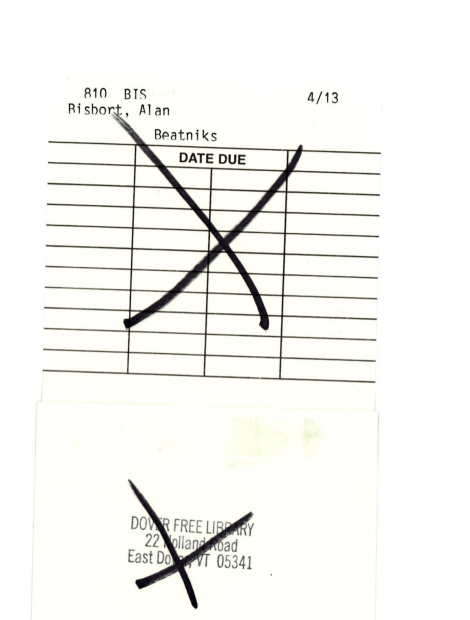